Powerdigm

DR JAYNE LIND

MONARCH
BOOKS
Mill Hill, London

First published in Great Britain 1998

British Library Cataloguing Data
A catalogue record for this book is available
from the British Library.

ISBN 1 85424 395 0

Designed and produced by Bookprint Creative Services
P.O. Box 827, BN21 3YJ, England for
MONARCH BOOKS
in association with
ANGUS HUDSON LTD
Concorde House, Grenville Place, Mill Hill
London NW7 3SA.
Printed in Great Britain.

To Edward,
Without whom this book would not have
been possible.

ACKNOWLEDGMENT

I want to thank Tony Collins, managing editor of Monarch Books, for his belief in this book, his help, and his encouragement.

CONTENTS

INTRODUCTION

Outside my window is a tree that loses its leaves every winter. But it doesn't lose them all at once. Some fall when the first strong wind blows; others drop off gradually as the autumn progresses. And some are so tenacious they stay till the very end; they are the last to drop to the ground.

I watch my tree as it grows thinner, and wonder about those leaves that hang on, buttressing themselves against the elements. Why do some appear to be so much stronger? Aren't all leaves created equal? They all look alike to me, but obviously, they are not all alike. Some are stronger than others; some are much more connected to the tree. Others evidently have a fragile hold on life and are not able to withstand much hardship.

Human beings are not so different from the leaves on my tree. Some, who look like all the others, who may even look better on the outside, don't weather storms too well. And others, who might not look as good to an outsider, have an inner strength that sustains them through almost anything.

This *inner strength*, *inner power*, is what we need. Inner power makes all the difference in those who are secure in this world, secure in their social interactions with others and secure within themselves.

When using the word 'power' in this book, I am speaking of inner power, inner strength. Power, both positive and negative, exists. We can't see it, but we feel it. If we think of power in a positive sense, a sense of 'being filled up,' then lack of power is just the opposite; it is a sense of emptiness, of having no strength.

We seek to be filled, to obtain power, in many ways, often unconsciously. We seek power through our accomplishments, through material acquisitions, and through our relationships. But power is often elusive and sometimes, when we have successfully climbed to the top in our career, or have attained financial security, or married the person we want, we still feel unsatisfied.

We are striving, not thriving, living in the future rather than the present. We look forward to an event like a birthday, a trip, or the completion of a project and when the event happens, when we attain or finish something, it does not feel as good as we thought it would. The happiness turns out to be temporary, fleeting. Many of us become disillusioned when our goals are reached, become upset with ourselves; we ask ourselves why we are never happy and we probably blame others as well. What's wrong with us? What is wrong with us, at least many of us, is that we feel powerless in numerous areas of our lives, powerless inside and therefore outside.

It is my belief and the belief of many who work in the mental health field that inner power comes from feeling loved, ideally as a child, and then continuously throughout life. Being loved as a child gives our personalities a good foundation; we are started on the right foot, so to speak. Those who have been filled with the power of love are power *full* and have little need to struggle for power. Those who are not filled are either 'power empty' or feel power-less in many situations.

Just as one way of looking at the universe is by under-standing the laws of physics which govern our planet, one way our actions, personalities, and motivations can be seen is through the concept of power and/or lack of power. Without inner power, there can be no inner peace.

Christ said, 'Peace I leave with you; my peace I give you' (John 14:27) Do you experience that peace? Do you know what he meant by those words? In many churches, Sunday after Sunday, the service ends with the blessing, 'May the peace of God which passes all understanding, keep your hearts and minds in the knowledge and love of God and of his Son Jesus Christ our Lord.'[1]

'Peace that passes all understanding' – those words used to haunt me. What was that peace, I used to wonder? I now believe, based on my interpretation of the Scriptures and on what I know of human nature, that the inner peace Christ spoke of is the source of happiness.

Yet there are many who do not experience that peace, some because they do not have a personal relationship with Jesus Christ and others, who *are* Christians and want that peace very badly, but do not understand why they do not have it.

Nicholas, a postman in a small rural village, constantly finds himself struggling in relationships with others. Not only at home with his wife, but as he delivers his mail each day, it always seems to him the people he deals with criti-cise him and he gets angry. 'What do you mean the mail is late today! I'm exactly on time, well, maybe a few minutes late, but you shouldn't be just standing there waiting for me,' he says crossly. At home, he often finds himself trying to dominate his wife, to get his way. For Nicholas, life is one daily struggle.

Jeannette, on the other hand, is pleasant with others; she hardly ever has a confrontation with anyone. Because she is smiling and co-operative, everyone thinks Jeannette a very nice person. But she still struggles. She struggles within herself. Jeannette has an eating disorder and for her, as for Nicholas, life is difficult.

Life can be one long struggle. One way to look at it is to regard life as a struggle for power. In interactions and inner actions, we struggle with someone else or struggle within ourselves. Either we are trying to overcome something about ourselves we do not like or we are striving for power in relation to others.

Whether the problem is a struggle within ourselves (for example, a problem with weight) or whether the problem is an exchange with another person (in which he or I come away feeling deflated) the dynamics are the same. If I continue to gain weight, I feel powerless in this aspect of my life; I will have an internal struggle and an internal dialogue that can be defined as a power struggle. In terms of interactions, whether it be with a spouse, a boss or any other relationship, there are times when we feel powerless. The more powerless we feel, the more we will struggle. And the more we struggle, the less we will have peace within.

This does not mean there are not balanced relationships, nor that there are not areas in our lives we have conquered, where we are in control, where we do have power. But many, if not most of us, encounter power struggles on a daily basis.

Besides wanting help with their emotional problems and wanting to know how to change themselves or their situations, clients in my practice always want to know why, why they did what they did, felt as they felt, and most of all, why they seem to repeat their past mistakes, particularly in relationships. In reviewing their childhood and sub-

sequent lives, we are often successful in pinpointing theor-
etical reasons for their behaviour. However, when I began
using the concept of either having power or not having
power, struggling to achieve power and/or giving up one's
power, the 'whys' became clearer.

This new paradigm for personality theory, *Powerdigm*,
as I have named it, gives me a useful method of helping
people understand why and how they got where they are.
A paradigm is a concept whereby one distinguishes a
pattern existing. I have looked at personalities and discovered a pattern involving either having power or not having
power – hence a paradigm for personality. This way of
looking at personality, the *Powerdigm* theory, is not the
only way to explore one's personality – it is simply a different and effective way.

In this book, I am combining psychological principles
with spiritual principles. We are spiritual beings, just as we
are psychological and physical beings. We are what we are
because God made us this way, so in speaking of things
psychological, I must intertwine them with the spiritual.

Paul said 'I do not understand what I do.' (Romans 7:15)
Hopefully, this book will help the reader understand his or
her own behaviour; hopefully, this book will tell you why
you do what you do.

The first three chapters of the book will help you understand the concepts of the *Powerdigm* theory. The fourth
chapter provides background about how our personalities
are formed. Subsequent chapters deal with specific topics
such as: male/female differences relating to power, relationships, depression, anxiety, addictions and anger. The
concluding chapter is about spiritual power, the most
lasting kind.

Chapter 1

POWER FULL AND POWER EMPTY

Power empty

Tom seemed to have everything he needed. He went to the best schools, then on to a prestigious university, followed by medical school. Gregarious, Tom had many friends; he certainly acted as if he were happy. But deep inside, Tom felt hollow, empty. He put up a good front; he became successful; he worked hard, and it wasn't until his marriage broke up and he went into therapy that he began to admit how powerless he felt.

Tall and well built, Tom reminded me of the pictures in *Gentlemen's Quarterly*: impeccable looks and impeccable clothes. One would never know from looking at him on the outside that anything was wrong.

'I don't understand why I've always felt something was missing,' he told me. 'My parents are wonderful people; they gave me everything I wanted. You hear about all these poor kids who are abused, whose parents are alcoholics, all those terrible things. I had nice parents. They never did anything wrong!'

However, as I got to know more about Tom, a picture

began to develop of a very lonely little boy in a big house with two people who were indeed very 'nice,' not only to Tom, their only child, but to everyone. They gave Tom everything they were capable of giving him. His parents didn't lose their temper; he wasn't criticised; they were not overly strict; but neither did he see a lot of smiles, or laughter, or affection. The picture that began to emerge was of a home in black and white. No colour.

Although Tom's parents had given him everything he could want in material ways, they had not given him the inner power that only comes from being loved. Not because they didn't want to and not because he wasn't loveable, but because they simply did not know how. So Tom went along trying to earn what he instinctively knew was missing, trying to earn love, trying to be filled up.

Power full

Maria, on the other hand, grew up in a poor section of a city, a very tough neighbourhood. She had to resist drugs and crime and she worked long hours after school at McDonald's. She had never known her father; Maria was born to a teenage mother whose boyfriend had refused to have anything to do with her when he found out she was pregnant.

But Maria had an inner peace. She was happy, cheerful, warm and loving. In the midst of the poor circumstances in which she grew up, Maria was given consistent love and acceptance by her mother. Maria and her mother were a solid family unit, bonded in a strong love for each other. Maria was filled with a positive force, a positive power; she was power full.

We all know people like Tom, who seem to have everything and yet are unhappy and, conversely, people like

Maria who have grown up with deprivation and yet seem to be secure, self-confident.

Princess Diana was the ultimate example of someone who looked good on the outside, had all the power outwardly one could want, yet must have felt empty inside. She was searching for love, struggling for the inner power of love, and tragically, seemed to have found that love only during the last months of her life.

Positive power

We start our life as empty vessels. It is true we are born with inherited predispositions toward different personality traits, but in the very beginning we are empty in terms of love. Think of a human being as an uncharged battery; we need to be charged. We can be charged with positive power or negative power or a mixture of both. If we label love as positive power and hate as negative power, it is apparent that what fills us makes a difference. If we were not filled with positive power as a child, as was Maria, or do not find, later in life, some one person who loves us enough to fill us with the power of love and/or do not experience the love of God through Christ, then we may feel empty or we may fill ourselves with negative power; emotions such as envy, hatred or anger.

Love is positive power, comparable to the power generated by electricity. Without it, our light does not shine, so to speak. We are dark. Without love, we feel powerless, empty of power. Just as an electrical cord that is not plugged into the wall is devoid of power, so are we without power unless or until we are hooked up.

When we love someone, we bestow power on that person; we literally give some of our power to that other person. We need God's love, but we also need love from others. Christ told us to love our neighbour as ourselves (Matthew 22:39). 'Love your neighbour as yourself' – I used to read these words and think of them only as an instruction to me, telling me what I was supposed to do. I am supposed to love my neighbour as myself. I now believe those words are also a clue that all of us need to *be* loved. God has created us in such a way that we need love, not just want it, but need it. Christ is telling us that for most of us the love of God alone is not enough; we each, individually, need to receive love from at least one other human being. This does not diminish God's love, it adds to it. By making sure we obey and love others, we are helping to fulfil God's intentions, his intention that everyone be loved by someone.

For some understanding of how important the emotion and commitment of love is to God, take a Bible concordance and look up the word 'love'. There is an enormous number of Scripture references to that word; it was an eye-opening experience for me.

Receiving love

There is a catch, however. Unless this love is received, it will not help. Love may be there, being offered, but often, because someone doesn't feel worthy and/or cannot believe that anyone would love him or her, and therefore is not open to accepting this love, it will not be received. There are those with personality problems, emotional and mental illnesses, who put up barriers to receiving love, even that which comes from God. There are those who have built up a defence and do not let anyone love them. Even though such people feel empty, they can receive no power from those who try to love them.

Empty power

The power that our accomplishments give us is either negative or neutral, empty, unable to fill us, and also temporary. It never lasts. Joe Morgan, the baseball star, was being
interviewed on the radio after having been inducted into
the Baseball Hall of Fame. 'It was a wonderful feeling!' he
told the interviewer. 'The height of my dreams!' He was
then asked, 'How long did that feeling last, Joe?' 'Oh, about
twenty minutes,' was the reply[2].

For all of us, whether we are power full or not, awards,
titles and money do not make a lasting impression in terms
of inner peace and strength. After attaining these, we very
often still feel power empty. In the case of a career, a title
may be given to us, or a pay rise, but we may not experience a feeling of real satisfaction. Most people who earn a
doctorate feel a let-down after their dissertation is completed; the elation they expected isn't there. After all that
hard work, where is the joy? We are puzzled, despairing,
often becoming depressed or anxious when we have
attained whatever it is we were seeking and find it so unsat-
isfactory. Is this all there is?

Someone, not something, must give us love. Objects do
not give us love; professional titles and positions do not give
us love. Both objects and titles do contain power, but not the
kind of power that satisfies us. Objects and titles can, and
often do, contribute to our self-esteem. Doing a job well and
having others recognise us for our hard work, talent and
intelligence does make us feel better about ourselves. Even
if no one gives us praise for a job well done or for having
gained financial security, these achievements certainly make
us feel better than being jobless or a failure. Yet after we have
accomplished what we were striving for, the achievements
and/or the praise and recognition often seem empty. In the

end, objects and positions alone are not enough to make us power full; we just will not be quite as empty.

High self-esteem vs. power full

Tom's life certainly fitted into this category. He had external power, lots of it. He had attained his goals and the financial security which one would think would make someone feel power full. He was good-looking, in fine health, well liked and respected by his colleagues. Tom also felt very good about himself; he was proud of his accomplishments and did not minimise them. Though not boastful, he did have high self-esteem.

I have used Tom's story because it so aptly illustrates the difference between high self-esteem and feeling power full. It is possible to have an honest, true self-appraisal that is positive; in other words, to have high self-esteem, and yet not be power full. Tom thought he was a good physician; he thought he was a sensitive and caring friend; he believed in himself; he had high self-esteem. But he still felt empty.

Tom blamed himself. He knew he was unhappy, but since nothing seemed to satisfy him, he finally decided he needed help. All his life he had set goals, and he, like most of us, assumed that when he finally reached his goals he would be content. He blamed his unhappiness on the fact that he was continually striving after one more achievement. When he finally got to the pinnacle and found that the magic of being happy was not there, he blamed himself for the feeling of dissatisfaction he experienced.

Over the years, I found many clients who expressed this same vague sense of restlessness. Most of the time these people were affluent, had families, interesting jobs and interesting pursuits. Yet there was a struggle for some undefined quality; since everything looked good on the outside, they inevitably felt they should be happy. 'Why am I not happy?' was often asked in the privacy of my office.

Happiness vs. peace

We all want to be happy. Happiness sounds like a noble goal, but I have come to believe that human beings are not constitutionally made always to be happy. Even when everything is wonderful, we do not seem able to sustain that feeling for long. It is then that we berate ourselves; we think we should be happy and we are not.

We do not often use the word *peace* to describe what it is we want out of life. Instead we use the word *happiness*. But I believe that is the turn in the road where we make our mistake. If we are seeking happiness, we can attach all kinds of labels to that word, different for everyone and different for each of us at any given time. But if we knew from the start that what we were seeking was inner peace, which would, in turn, bring us happiness, then our personal journey would be much more satisfying.

Feeling at peace within oneself is much more stable than the emotion of happiness. That is because inner peace starts within and manifests itself outwardly, whereas happiness depends on other people or things or events – therefore it begins outside of us and we expect it to make us feel good inside. Scripture does not promise us happiness, but it does promise us joy and peace. Inner peace is a state of calm, of serenity, of lack of struggle.

We can and often do 'struggle' to feel happy – that's what much drinking and drug-taking is – a struggle to feel exhilarated, even if only for a brief time. Pubs have 'happy hours' with drinks being less expensive – the connotation being, a time to get happy. A classic example of struggling to be happy is a New Year's Eve celebration. 'Let's whoop it up!' Let's celebrate! Many times there is actually a let-down at a time like that because we've built up our expectations; we think we should be happy at a time like that and often we are not.

A feeling of happiness comes when it comes; it won't come by artificially trying to make oneself happy. Peace, on the other hand, is stable; it is not transitory. A person who is at peace within him or herself has no need to struggle for a feeling of happiness.

Negative power – power struggles

Over and over again, I have listened to people in therapy say these exact words, 'I feel empty.' If we feel empty, if we feel a void in our life, we will seek to fill that void. When we feel power empty, we feel we have no control over our life. And if we have no control over our life, we feel insecure and will instinctively struggle to be 'filled up', to gain strength, power, often in negative ways.

The more powerless we feel, the more we are going to struggle for power. That is when the word 'power' begins to take on negative connotations. The struggle is negative, it is against other forces; it is pushing rather than working alongside. It leaves us and others around us with negative feelings.

Far too often, marriages become one long power struggle. Every therapist who does marriage counselling hears these words, 'I don't even remember what the fight was about!' Probably what the fight was about was a struggle for power. If couples are not equal in terms of feeling power full, if one or both of them feel empty, there usually will be a more or less constant struggle for power.

Roger and Shirley had been married for ten years, were the parents of two school-age children, and for the past five years had worked together; they owned and managed a small neighbourhood dry cleaners. On the surface, their working together appeared to be the problem. Until the younger child went to kindergarten, Shirley had stayed at home. While they don't remember their early years together as being idyllic, they agreed that it was not as bad then as now.

'She contradicts me all the time!' said Roger, with a grimace on his face. 'I can't do anything right in her eyes. No matter what I say to a customer or no matter what I do about a problem, she has something to say about it,' he went on. Shirley did not see it that way, of course. She felt that Roger was always putting her down, making her feel incompetent. 'He is so particular about everything. He looks over my shoulder and lots of times does something over again after I've done it.'

This couple, in their early forties, had come to marriage counselling out of a feeling of desperation. Neither of them liked conflict and yet their life had become one constant battle. As soon as they closed the shop, they reviewed the day, blaming each other for what each had done wrong. Of course, the resentment didn't start at the end of the day; it had been brewing quietly while other people were around. The minute Roger and Shirley were alone, a fight would erupt.

Neither of them had much self-confidence; neither of them felt power full. And since the majority of their day was spent at the shop, this shared work experience became their battleground. If they had worked at separate places, these eight hours spent together would not have provided the fuel for their power struggles, but they still would have argued. What was needed was to get to the root of their sense of emptiness, to lead each of them to an awareness of how the power struggle filled them with negative power. This negative power, unfortunately, often feels better than being empty.

Without getting into the details of this case, but simply describing their behaviour, these two people were engaging in what had become a constant power struggle. Each had a desperate need to get the better of the other one; each felt resentment until the other person was put in his or her place. I explained to them that they were competing with one another, competing for power.

There was much more work to be done on this marriage, but that explanation helped them a great deal. When I put a name on their behaviour and each of them began to see what they were doing as each incident happened, change began to occur.

A definition of power

The word 'power' is used very loosely and often has negative connotations. My dictionary's first definition is the faculty of doing or performing something. That does not sound negative; that sounds very ordinary. But it does imply motion, a sense of moving ahead. In contrast, the word 'powerless' presents images of standing still, being motionless. Power denotes strength. My thesaurus lists the words force and strength as synonyms for power. Some of the other words given are vigour, might, potency, authority, control, command, vitality, magnetism and mastery.

There are not as many synonyms given for the word 'powerlessness', but as one would expect, they all begin with the prefix in- (inability, incapability, inadequacy, ineffectiveness, impotent). When we feel powerless, we do feel incapable, inadequate, etc. And when we feel full of power, all those strong words listed above are true; we feel we can handle anything. Yet in actuality, we may have power at times and feel powerless at other times, according to what area of our life we are referring.

Power continuum

Very few things in life are black or white, one extreme or the other. Most concepts can be placed on a continuum, rather than being either/or. If total power is at one end of the continuum and lack of power at the other, total power represents the number 100 and no power at all would be 0.

POWER EMPTY   POWER FULL
0 100

With this graphic image in mind, it can be seen that hardly anyone is at either end of this spectrum. Everyone is at some point on the continuum. And not only that, everyone is at a different point on the continuum in relation to different people and different circumstances.

A man may be about a 65 on the power continuum at his office. He may be in charge of many people (and therefore has power over them). He may be entrusted with important decisions every day; his judgement may mean the difference between financial profit or loss to his company. Or other people's welfare may be entrusted to him; his decisions, skill and ability impact other people's lives.

Yet this man may be about a 20 in his relationship with his wife. She may have almost total power over him. Not necessarily in the sense of the stereotypical henpecked husband; she may have power over him because he has her on a pedestal, is so much in love with her that he believes she can do no wrong – this gives her power. Or she may be physically ill; this gives people a lot of power. Whether her illness is real or not does not matter in terms of power; the fact that she is ill could make him give in to her when he would rather not, perhaps stay with her when he would rather not. Any of these factors and many more could hypothetically affect the difference between his place on the continuum in his work as opposed to his relationship with his wife.

A teenager may feel power full at home; she may have loving parents and feel good about herself in relation to her family. But this same student might have many doubts about herself at school; she may have to struggle all the time to keep up with her peers academically and could label herself as powerless, when actually it is only in that one area that she is powerless.

So we need to categorise, separate the areas of our lives and not give ourselves or others a blanket appraisal of having power or being powerless; we are each on a different point on the continuum, depending upon the relationship to which we are referring. Those who are power *full*, especially those who received this gift of love from birth on, are much more stable in terms of the continuum of power. They seem much more content than others might who are always struggling to get higher on the continuum.

* * *

If the *Powerdigm* theory of positive and negative power, plus the concept of power struggles, either within ourselves or with others, strikes a chord within you, this book will help bring you to an understanding of yourself. I am convinced that understanding has to come first. My purpose is to lead the reader into the realm of identification, of solving the mysteries deep within him or herself.

Power full and power empty are feelings, feelings which can and do shape how we feel about ourselves and others. A power struggle is the name of the process; it describes what happens. Not every idea, not every situation, is for every reader; but each may find his or her story in the stories of others. However, the overall concepts of understanding yourself or others in your life, the theory of either being power full or power empty, or somewhere in between on the continuum; the theory of positive power and negative power applies to everyone. We have all had negative experiences; the amount and the intensity of those experiences are what make the difference.

Habits and emotions can be changed; behaviour can be changed. There are many people in the Church who have personal as well as personality problems, sincere believers who do not understand why they do the things they do (like Paul!). Hopefully, this book will be a beginning for the process of a more power-filled life. And there are many who are still searching for God, who may not even know that is what their sense of emptiness is about. Knowing why, naming the problem, redefining what is missing or what is wrong, all these make change less difficult to accomplish.

There are many circumstances as well as interactions that can be defined as power fillers and power drainers, events which sometimes change the very course of our lives. Negative emotions, negative interactions, drain us of power; the power of love recharges us, fills us. The next two chapters will deal with these factors.

CHAPTER 2

POWER DRAINERS

There are events that fill us with power, make us feel good about ourselves, on top of the world, and there are others that have the opposite effect – there are incidents that literally drain us, rob us of power. Even if someone is power full, there are situations that can be temporarily draining and for those who are not power full, power-draining situations such as interactions within one's family can often be deadly, affecting them for many years afterward.

An example of how family interactions can deeply impact people was brought home to me as I watched a young Mexican-American man, who is in prison for robbery, being interviewed on television. The programme was about the plight of teens who break the law. He recalled a time in high school when he made the decision to change his habits and began to study for the first time.

'I got an A on my report card! I was so proud,' he said, smiling as he remembered the feeling. 'But my brothers and sisters, when I told them, they said I was a nerd. And then I took the report card to my mother and she said, "Oh, that's nice."'

This young man smiled during the entire interview; he

never looked sad. I, however, felt very sad as I was watching, because when this event is viewed in light of the *Powerdigm*, his disappointment was an enormous power drainer. He felt good, filled with some power, when he got that first A, maybe as much as he had ever been. Internally, he had gained some positive power, but externally, in his interactions, he had gained nothing. The reaction of indifference he received to his achievement was like the pricking of a balloon; it was a pivotal turning point, a supreme power drainer.

I am sure this one event did not thrust him into criminal acts, yet he had obviously gone on to seek power in other, more negative ways. If there had been some reinforcement, no matter how little, for that wondrous report card, if someone had been as proud of him as he was of himself, the event would have been power filling rather than power draining. It may sound reckless to state that one event, one power-draining incident or conversely, one power-filling incident, can determine how one's life will go. Yet over and over in therapy, I have had clients tell me that there was a turning point; one event had changed their lives, for better or for worse.

We want to be right

Putting daily interactions into the *Powerdigm* has helped me to understand many behaviours, in myself as well as others. In any interaction there is a desire, conscious or not, to be the one who is right. Even if we know we are wrong, yet win the interaction, we gain some power. Not positive power – this kind of filling up will never make anyone power full, but it usually feels better than losing. Why do we have such a need to be right? Why does that demon of obstinacy rise up in us when someone tells us we are wrong? Because it is experienced as a power struggle and in power struggles, we either win or we lose. If we lose, we have lost power or at least that's how it may feel and how it may be interpreted. If we win, we feel we have gained some power.

I was writing in my office one day when a colleague came in to say hello. I explained the theme of this book to him and he said the concept intrigued him. He went on to say that he had a friend who was a scriptwriter in Hollywood. 'Whenever we watch a scene on TV together, after two people have had a conversation, my friend says "Who won that?"' In other words, who ended up on top in terms of power? This scriptwriter knew about power struggles; she was referring to the same concept as am I.

We want to be right. We don't want to be wrong. Being right, winning the point, is a power filler. When a person gets the better of someone, there is a sense of power. Perhaps there is also a sense of anger; perhaps the relationship is weakened rather than strengthened, but the person who gets the last word does gain a sense of power, negative power. When someone says 'I took him down a peg or two,' what that person is really saying is, 'I put myself up a peg or two,' gained some power, albeit negative power. However, the other person in the interaction will experience this as a power drainer, unless that person happens to be self-confident enough to see the interaction for what it is.

I had a professor in college who fascinated me in terms of her ability to cope with whatever came up in the classroom. My observation was that she never, ever became defensive. When someone in the class would challenge her or disagree with her she would smile or laugh and carry on a discussion with that person in such a positive way that the result was disarming. She was so sure of herself, so apparently power filled, that she did not need to 'prove' anything to anyone about herself. She was confident in her knowledge and ability, but there was more than that; her personality was such that arguments were not power draining for her; they were not a set-back. She simply handled the situation, made her point, and at the same time, did not make the student feel folish for doubting her statements. It was a pleasure to watch, a role model for anyone who was studying the dynamics going on, certainly a lesson for me.

Criticism

Criticism is a very effective power drainer. There are very few of us self-confident enough to ignore criticism. Humiliation is a deeper and even more destructive form of criticism, more power draining. I so often see and hear interactions between parents and children in which the child is unbelievably humiliated, so much so that it makes me cringe. The damage done to a child's self-esteem, the powerlessness of the child (usually a small child) is so devastating that it is hurtful to watch.

The expression 'taking the wind out of his sails' is a graphic example of a power-draining interaction. We win and lose these every day, but there are people who feel they lose them all and others who have an intense need to win them all. Whenever power is extended outward to power over someone or something else, it can become destructive. The classic power struggle begins.

I only know Sam through what his wife, Sheila, tells me. Sam would never come in for therapy, not even for one session so that I could meet him. From hearing Sheila's side of the story, it appears that Sam engages in power struggles with whomever he meets, at home, on the job, or with anyone who 'gets in his way'. He has to be the expert, no matter what the topic of conversation, and if the other person doesn't immediately agree with him, he begins haranguing and putting the other person down. Of course, this leads to frequent job changes and not having friends and a horrendous marriage. Why is he this way? Why start something every time you meet someone?

All I can do is guess, since Sam isn't about to let someone like me talk to him. My educated guess is that Sam is very, very angry, that his anger was born in childhood, that his father probably treated him exactly as he now treats others, and that the negative power he fills himself with by 'winning' these self-imposed arguments is all he has to go on. This negative power is his fuel. He is probably very empty and knows no other way to fill himself up. It is sad, but there are many Sams in the world, needing help, needing to be off their guard long enough to let someone love them, to be filled up, and yet who usually remain as they are all their lives.

Competition

Competition can often be seen as a power struggle. Competition is about being filled with power or drained of power. The best one wins – not just the prize or the game, but power also. Winning makes one feel more powerful; losing makes one feel less powerful. Competitions do not have to be large; they do not have to be either positive or negative. Sam turns every conversation, every incident, into a competition, but on a more subtle level, all of us have to compete at times. How one accepts the results depends upon whether one is power full or power empty or somewhere in between. A power-full person can have a competitive spirit in a very healthy manner. He can play a set of tennis, or bid on a job, or run for office with all his resources and can accept the results without anger (if it is a loss) and without arrogance (if it is a win). Competition is present every day for all of us, but for some, if there is not a win, it is experienced as a drainage of power.

Imagination

Our imagination has the potential to be a power drainer. Negative thoughts can actually make us feel down, sad, depressed, or just worse than we did before we thought about something unfavourable. If what we are thinking is true, rational, then the negative feelings probably cannot be helped, but if our imagination builds a scenario that isn't true, then our imagination can get us into trouble.

Let's imagine a scenario to illustrate the point. Jerry is walking down the street and sees Tiffany, one of the real beauties in the school. She is in his maths class this term. He begins to imagine that she is going to look at him, smile, and say hello. His imagination continues, goes on and on, building a movie-type love scene. Jerry feels happy inside. Here she comes; she's getting close; she's going to see him and break out in a big smile any minute now! Tiffany, unaware of Jerry's imagination and in reality, unaware of Jerry at all, walks right by him without noticing him. Jerry is crestfallen. He feels terrible. He had filled himself with power using his imagination and now he feels drained, upset, even a little bit angry at Tiffany. He shouldn't be angry at the girl, of course; it isn't her fault he feels this way. His imagination had pulled his feelings down; his imagination caused him to build expectations that were unrealistic; his imagination became a power drainer. We all often do this kind of thing to ourselves, drain ourselves of power needlessly.

Worry

Worry is a power drainer. Worry is a form of fear, a form of anxiety. Scripture tells us 'an anxious heart weighs a man down' (Proverbs 12:25). Yet we do get anxious; we do worry about all kinds of things.

Indecision is an example of a power drainer. When we don't know what to do, the manifestation of not knowing what to do is to worry. If we don't know what is going to happen, and if we let that indecision, fear of the unknown, worry us, we can be drained of a great deal of our power. Worse yet, anxiety and fear can make us feel so powerless that we can't think straight and become paralysed, unable to use what resources we do have to solve the problem.

Worry is the antithesis of trust. Jesus told us not to worry; he said not to worry about shelter, food, clothing and health (Matthew 6:25–34). How much of what we worry about has to do with those four things? We worry about having the money to buy a house, to keep the house up, to furnish it, to redecorate it. We buy a new coat when we already have three and then we worry about the credit card bill. We overeat and then worry about our weight. And we worry about our health. We worry, even though Jesus said that we could not, by worrying, add one hour to our life.

Worry is a power-draining emotion that we could gain control of by not overextending ourselves financially and by learning to trust God to take care of us. Simplistic? Yes. Jesus was telling us to keep it simple – but we don't. Instead, we complicate our lives in unbelievable ways; we drain ourselves of power by buying more than we can afford, by wanting more than we need, and then worrying about the consequences. I am not throwing the first stone; I too am guilty of not keeping my life simple.

Guilt

Power comes in many disguises. Some, who may feel pow-erless, actually have a great deal of power. The story of Joe and Kathy is one illustration.

Joe is a successful salesman for a company that makes machine tools. He had been married for over twenty years and had wanted to end the marriage for at least the past ten years. The relationship with his wife, Kathy, had been acrimonious from the beginning until finally they had both ceased to care enough to fight and had settled into a quiet, dull life. Very little was said when Joe finally came home in the evening and weekends were spent away as much as he could manage, usually playing golf. They were, in the true sense of the word, living together. Sex had long ago terminated; they were legally married but lived as room-mates.

Kathy was as unhappy as Joe, but having no confidence in her ability to attract another husband and knowing that she did not want to live alone, she let year after year drag on, as did Joe. Joe had indulged himself in a few affairs, but there had never been any emotional attachment.

Then things changed. They changed because Joe met someone with whom he had a great deal in common, someone who came to work for his company, and he fell in love. Kathy soon found out about the affair and after a bitter fight, Joe moved out. Kathy became severely depressed, threatened suicide, and Joe moved back in.

Nothing had changed; Kathy was still depressed and Joe was still attached to the other woman. One night, in a rage, he packed his bags again. Kathy became more depressed and again threatened suicide. This cycle played itself out over and over again, with Joe eventually refusing to move back in when he realised that she had never really attempted suicide; but every time he talked of divorce, even though he was now living with the other woman, Kathy again said she would kill herself.

Power. She had and was using one of the strongest powers available, emotional blackmail. And it worked for her. Joe was a decent guy and he certainly didn't want her to kill herself; he could not summon the nerve to take the gamble. Who could blame him? So three people's lives were miserable, drained of power.

Emotional blackmail is a longer way to say guilt. Making someone feel guilty is a way to gain power by the accuser. Why would someone, why do we, want to make someone feel guilty? Because it is one way of gaining power, not positive power, but power, nevertheless. When guilt is used as a hold on someone, it is an effort to gain control and make the other person change. As long as Joe kept moving back in, the guilt was working; he felt powerless in this situation. Guilt can be a supreme power drainer.

If Kathy had been willing to give up this negative power, give up making Joe feel guilty, she might have gone on with her life. If she had sought other relationships, she might have found someone who really loved her, someone who could make her power full. Either no one explained it to her in quite these terms, or if they did, she was not able or willing to relinquish this hold on Joe, this power-draining situation. I am not condoning Joe's behaviour; there was obviously blame on both sides for the failure of this marriage. It is too bad this couple did not seek help for their marriage years earlier, when it probably could have been saved.

We instinctively try to gain power when we are empty – much like water seeking its own level – and, in a pathological way, some people will do everything they can to make everyone around them feel guilty. Mothers of grown-up children are famous for this. ('You never phone me', says Mum in a complaining voice. 'Mum, I phoned you last week.' 'Well – it seems like it was a lot longer than that.')

Why? Why would this mother, these mothers, we, all of us, want to make someone feel guilty? This son would be much more eager to phone his mother if he were not going to be admonished each time he did it. He probably does not call as often because of her guilt-inducing statements. Why be so self-defeating? Because when making someone feel guilty works, it gives the guilt-inducer some power over the one he or she is making feel guilty; when it works, he or she is gaining negative power – which feels better than being empty.

Losses

Divorce and death of a loved one are two of the most power-draining events that can happen to people. Each can create a sense of being powerless, sometimes desperately powerless. In the case of a death, the fact that there is nothing that can be done to bring the person back can bring on overwhelming feelings of having no power. In death there is no hope, and loss of hope is a serious drainage of power.

Divorce can be just as devastating; the spouse who did not want the divorce will often feel desperately powerless, to the point of depression. In the case of divorce, on some level of consciousness, there may be hopes, albeit these hopes may be delusions, that the other person will come back.

Losing one's job is a clear example of a circumstantial power drainer. A job gives a person much more than money; it gives him or her power, power to exert some control over his or her life. The anxiety caused by being unable to provide for one's family or for oneself, plus the fear of the future, brings on much negative thinking and either self-recrimination or anger. Whichever of these negative emotions is having its way, the results are a loss of power.

The empty nest syndrome is another example of a loss of power. A mother has some amount of power over her children. If this is her only source of power, she feels empty when it is gone.

A happy resolution to this empty nest syndrome occurred a few years ago with a woman I saw in therapy for what appeared to be mild depression. Nancy was in her mid-fifties, pleasantly plump, with just a few touches of grey in her hair. She was not only pleasantly plump, she was pleasantly everything. From her perspective, she had lived a very satisfactory life, bringing up four children, with only a minor problem now and then. Her life had revolved around them. She was the classic caretaker; doing things for them brought her much pleasure. So what was the problem?

The problem was that one by one her children had grown up and moved away. Jobs, school and circumstances had dictated that they live in different parts of the country. For the first time in her married life, Nancy had no one to 'do for'. It wasn't that she did not do things for her husband, but he was still in the prime of his career and there were no financial worries. There was no reason for her to cook every night, about half the time they had dinner in nice restaurants and his shirts were done better in the laundry, thank you.

Nancy's problem was that she had lost her role. Just as surely as if her husband had been made redundant by his company at the age of fifty-five, she had been made redundant from her job. She had no idea what to do with herself;

she had formed her identity around her family. Classic empty nest.

'I feel so useless,' she told me. 'Going to lunch with my friends was fine when I had a real job at home, but I need to be useful!' Nancy was one of those clients who are easy to work with in therapy. She was basically emotionally healthy and certainly was not power empty, but these circumstances, being without children who had been the centre of her universe, these circumstances had become power draining.

If her husband had also retired, I am sure they would have travelled and had an interesting new life. Often, however, the mother retires first. We explored options such as returning to college for a graduate degree, or taking computer courses, but none of those really appealed to Nancy. After six months of floundering around, trying one thing and then another, Nancy went to work at a small, fashionable dress boutique. She had good taste in clothes and her easy, affable manner made her very popular with the women who patronised the shop. Nancy was perfect for the job. These customers did not want a saleswoman who dressed in mini-skirts and reminded them they weren't getting any younger. Nancy was able to 'do for' these women. They became her new nest; she no longer felt useless, powerless; she blossomed in her new role.

Illness

When people are chronically ill, unless and until they are able to change their outlook, their perception of the disease or injury, they may feel powerless. The disease is the powerful one, they are not. Unless they are able to get the better of the disease by a change in attitude, by taking control of their regimen, by not blindly following the statistics of doom, they will continue to feel powerless.

There are no more courageous examples of this than the cancer survivors who have decided to fight their disease rather than give into it. My husband, Edward, is one such person from whom I have learned much about being power full.

In 1988 he had a suspicious-looking mole removed; it was diagnosed as being a malignant melanoma. The area was excised deeply and he was told to have frequent check-ups, which he did. In February of the next year, it was found that the malignancy had spread to the lymph glands and surgery was again done to remove the nodes. Then, in April, he found out about a research study on melanoma being done at the M.D. Anderson Hospital in Houston, Texas and flew there to join the study. During the physical examination before his being accepted as part of the study, the doctors decided that his prior surgery had not been extensive enough and so surgery was done again and more nodes were found. He was assured that this time all the malignancy had been removed and therefore no chemotherapy was recommended.

Up to this point, the story sounds fairly familiar. The only initiative Edward had taken on his own was to try to get on the research study, which we believe led to the saving of his life. In other words, no one had recommended he do this; he was willing to do anything to prevent the illness from controlling his life.

After this second scare, he really began to take charge. He went to the Livingston Clinic, an immunology centre that advocates building up the immune system to fight cancer. The clinic is not in any way a competition for traditional medicine; in fact, to be a patient there one must also be seeing an oncologist. The treatment he received consisted of being put on a healthy diet, taking different vitamins and minerals, and most importantly, meditating once a day, instructing the cells in his body to fight any intruding cancer cells, relaxing and giving his body positive messages. He never gave up; he refused to become powerless over the disease. He did this by taking charge.

He or I do not know which one of the above remedies has resulted in his good health today; the answer is probably all of them. Yet he could have reacted differently; he could have looked at the statistics of those with metastasised melanoma and given up; he could have let the disease be the powerful one, but he didn't, he gained the upper hand as many others have done.

What Edward has done for himself and what physicians like Bernie Siegel have done through books and seminars on taking charge of one's medical programme is give people a sense of hope. Hope is a tremendous power filler; lack of hope is a power drainer.

*   *   *

From these few examples, it can be seen that negative emotions and negative situations are power drainers. Positive emotions, positive circumstances are power fillers. The next chapter turns to the more positive aspects of power.

CHAPTER 3

POWER FILLERS

Now that we have an idea about the actions and circumstances that drain us of power, what about the positive side of power, what incidents or inner actions or circumstances are able to fill us with power?

Temporary power fillers

Acquisitions

Having things, acquiring things is a power filler, but the good feelings are very temporary; the happiness they bring usually doesn't last.

New clothes, the latest styles, are objects or means that women often use to feel power full. Women are not usually competing with each other for men, much of the time they are competing for the power that comes from being the top of the heap in terms of the females, analogous to the strongest boy, or the man with the most toys. The majority of the time, in most women, this is unconscious. It is not that women want to win by being the best dressed, it is the confidence, the power, which comes from being well dressed that women seek. Being well dressed is a very real, although temporary method of feeling power full. At the very least, women want to avoid the feeling of powerlessness and this often is avoided by confidence provided by new clothes.

I have always felt that uniforms for school children and for employees provide a safe, comfortable manner in which to dress. It relieves all the worry about competition and having just the right thing to wear. Saying uniforms are a power filler may be stretching it, but they do, often, prevent power-draining situations.

Shopping is also a tremendous power filler for both genders. Buying something, the actual act of having the money (or the credit card) to purchase something is, for some, a very real (temporary) way to feel better, to feel filled up. It does not matter what we buy and it does not matter whether it is something we really need, whether it is just filling up the pantry with a week's worth of groceries or buying new curtains or a new car, the power comes from being able to buy it. If money is something a person cannot handle, if buying becomes an addiction or, on a lesser scale, creates problems with debt, then the good feeling felt at the time of purchase very soon becomes a power drainer. The worry or self-recrimination leads to guilt, which is always a power drainer.

Men often derive power from their cars. This phenomenon, not always understood by women, is comparable to women's new clothes. Just as a woman is wrapped in a good-looking package when she puts on her new outfit, a man often feels 'wrapped up' in a new package when he is in his car. The car does what he wants it to do; it encompasses him, gives him a sense of power. A new car or new clothes will not make us power full; these new accoutrements will not keep us happy (else why would we need to keep buying new clothes and new cars)? This power is not from within, yet anything that makes us feel good can be a temporary power filler. That's the problem; it is only temporary.

Mastery

Why have so many people fallen in love with computers? Because computers do what we tell them to do (most of the time). There is something thrilling, power filling, about giving commands with your fingers and presto! The result is there, right on the screen. A sense of mastery that comes from learning any skill gives us a sense of power.

The control over his body that a good athlete has makes him feel more powerful, and the reverse of this is true – not having control over one's body can lead to a sense of powerlessness. Golfers speak of the thrill of hitting the perfect golf shot; equestrians know the thrill (infusion of power) of having perfect control over the horse; gymnasts experience a great deal of satisfaction as well as power by having such mastery over their bodies. These kinds of power-filling experiences, skills, can make us feel better about ourselves; they can help to build self-esteem. Yet we will not gain inner peace or even long-term happiness from mastering anything. If we are not power full, a restlessness will continue to surface from time to time.

Laughter and joy

Laughter and joy are power fillers. When we laugh, we take positive power down into ourselves; our entire body experiences laughter; we feel good, filled up for that moment. I like the old-fashioned word 'mirth'; it seems to epitomise the way I feel when I am struck by something as being funny. Norman Cousins wrote a book entitled *Anatomy of an Illness* in which he relates his discovery of the value of laughter when he was ill; he watched Laurel and Hardy movies because they made him laugh and he began to notice that he felt better after laughing.[3] We now know that laughter promotes the production of endorphins, the 'feel good' neurochemical in our brain. Another way to say we feel good is to say we are filled up, filled with good feelings, filled with power. I agree with his observation. Laughter can fill us with a very temporary feeling of well being, of joy, of happiness, but that feeling soon goes away, we can't sustain it, and I believe we aren't supposed to be able to sustain it. It is transitory, a little boost, a filler, but not permanent.

Joy is another old-fashioned word, not heard so often these days, but very descriptive of what we experience when we are so happy about something that we feel filled with power. Joy, like laughter, is transitory, sometimes only fleeting. C. S. Lewis speaks of experiencing 'the joy' in his diaries, but he always describes it as a momentary, almost elusive feeling.[4] Writing about his conversion to Christ after being an agnostic all his life, he wrote about his conversion experience and titled the book *Surprised by Joy*.[5]

The Bible is full of references to joy. Christ told his disciples that if they obeyed his commands, they would remain in his love and if they did that, their joy would be complete (John 15:10–11). Paraphrasing this verse, if I truly love Christ (with all my heart and with all my soul and with all my mind) it would follow naturally that I would obey him. Do we really love him in this way? If we struggle with Christ to have our own way, then we are not truly loving him and if we are not truly loving him, if we are struggling for power over our lives with him, then we are not obeying him. Hence, we may not experience joy.

What is the difference between the word 'happy' and the word 'joy'? Joy has the connotation of 'rejoice'. We do not go around rejoicing all the time; it is a temporary feeling when we are very glad about something. Whereas the word 'happy' seems to have come to mean a state we are in – we are either happy or we are not. People are said to have a happy marriage or a bad marriage. In reality, in the best of marriages, the couple is probably not 'happy' all the time, but there will be moments of joy and there will be a feeling of peace from within. So joy is a temporary emotion, a temporary power filler.

Praise

One of the mightiest ways to receive or give power is praise. Have you ever been given a compliment for something you have done that just 'makes you feel good all over'? Praise is a potent power filler, just as criticism was mentioned as a power drainer. Genuine, sincere praise is one of the nicest, most loving things we can do for people, especially people who need it, who don't seem to be power full. Small children who are given a lot of praise thrive under it, grow from it; it gives them confidence to keep on trying, to maybe even excel.

One day, my husband was out by our garage, near a paved area. An eleven or twelve-year-old boy, a bit overweight, was trying to ride a skateboard. Edward said he was terrible at it; he had no co-ordination. The boy realised Edward was watching him and stopped, self-conscious. Edward immediately said, 'You're doing pretty well on that thing!' The boy looked at him, surprised, and said, 'Yeah?' He went right back to trying, it seemed to Edward with more zest. Just a little praise, just a little bit of power filling, goes a long way.

Power fillers that endure

Belonging

An example of an enduring power filler is familiarity. When we are with those who are like us, we are comfortable; familiarity breeds power. When we are with those who are like us, we feel more in control, more understood, and therefore have more power than when we are with those who are different from us. The theme song of the popular television series in America, *Cheers*, includes the phrase, 'A place where everyone knows your name'. It feels good; we feel welcome in a place where everyone knows our name.

Many go to church out of a need to belong somewhere, to belong to some group, and church is often the one place some lonely people do belong. However, it is really sad when someone does not feel included in church and gives up going. One of Jesus' main messages was to love one another. Loving one another includes making people feel they belong. Unfortunately, some people may be made to feel they belong in a pub, while not being made to feel that way in a church.

Long before the territorial, destructive gangs we see today, teens formed clubs, had clubhouses, invited some kids in and kept others out. Fraternities and sororities are of the same ilk; it feels good to be invited in; belonging to a group gives us power that we don't have as an outsider.

The musical *Oliver!* graphically illustrates this principle. Oliver Twist, an orphan, runs away to London and is immediately taken to Fagin's home. Oliver did not know the boys were thieves; he simply felt so welcomed, 'one of the family' as one of the show's songs describes it, that he felt happier than he had ever been. He belonged, and in this belonging he did not feel so utterly powerless as he had all his life. Oliver had never experienced being loved, and pathetically, this inclusion, this acceptance into Fagin's gang, was his first gulp of the fresh air of caring. To someone so devoid of love, this was heart-filling and he was happier than he had ever been – he belonged.

Purpose

Any sense of banding together for a cause, a project, or even a job, also has the potential to make those who participate power full.

When the city of Berlin was divided after World War II, Russia was in control of the east side and the Western allies were in charge of the west. Many families were separated by the wall and could only wave from a window in a high-storied building to relatives on the free side. There is a museum today across the street from the famous Checkpoint Charlie, the only gate where passage between the two sides of the city was allowed, and then only under tight Russian control.

Many escape stories are related in this museum; the most poignant to me being the story of eight 'old people' who dug a tunnel and walked to their freedom. Tunnels were being dug from many buildings on the east side, dug under the road and into buildings on the other side. These projects entailed much planning and co-operation among the participants; the work was usually done at night and provisions had to be made for the disposal of the earth that was dug up each night. This group of senior citizens, the oldest being in his eighties, were told they could not be part of a tunnelling group going on a few houses away. The man in charge of this tunnel, told them, 'My tunnel is so low that you old people wouldn't be able to get through. Or you'll start gasping for breath and not survive.' What to do?

These men and women could have sat there in despair;

having no purpose in life, no hope and no occupation. Instead, they decided to dig their own tunnel! All of them participated in the digging, except for the oldest man, who, day after day, pretended to be an ardent gardener and while pruning and repruning his roses, was on the lookout for the East German soldiers. Meanwhile, the rest patiently dug, day after day, night after night. The earth was piled in a disused hen house after it had been drawn up in buckets on a rope by arm. Not satisfied just to escape, to build just any tunnel, this spirited group of 'old people' wanted to be able to walk upright, holding their heads high when they gained their freedom. They also wanted to get even with their neighbour after his insult. So they built a tunnel high enough for them to be able to walk out upright.

And that's what they did! One night, all eight walked to the West, upright, free to join their families, free to go any-where they liked. This project, this goal, had filled each of these people with power. It had given them energy, stamina and determination. After their safe arrival, they main-tained that work on the tunnel had made each of them ten years younger. It is a wonderful example of a power-filling event.[6]

Being understood

Before the ideas for this book came to me, I had planned to write a book some day entitled *What Everyone Wants Most of All Is To Be Understood.* Being understood gives us a sense of power; being understood can be and often is a glorious moment in a person's life, power filling. When someone really understands you, maybe for the first time, you may feel more power full than ever before. The story of the young Mexican-American man in the last chapter would have perhaps ended differently if just one person in his family had understood how much effort had gone into his achieving an A; if one person had been as proud of him as he was of himself, that moment in time could have turned into a power filler, rather than a power drainer. When we don't have much power anyway, when we are far down the scale on the continuum of power, it doesn't even take something as significant as what happened in this story to drain us, to make us feel completely empty.

Being understood is one of the main reasons why good therapy works. For far too many people, coming into therapy is the first time they have ever really been listened to, and from there, really understood. It is such a relief! Keeping problems and sorrows locked up inside consumes a great deal of negative energy. When that is all let out, when everything has been said, it feels better. But to have the added bonus of someone understanding how you feel; to have another human being empathetic enough to put him or herself in your place and share your agony – what a powerful power filler that is!

Most good therapists grow to care deeply for their clients. Actually, all of us would grow to care deeply for anyone whom we knew on the level that occurs in this relationship. Sadly, in our normal life, we do not take the time to know each other on that level and our friends, relatives, co-workers and acquaintances do not confide in us on that level. Why? Because revealing our innermost thoughts and feelings to another puts us at risk, puts us in the very vulnerable position of being one down. The person, be it friend or therapist, who knows everything about you has power over you. That is why the confidentiality of the therapy relationship feels safer.

It was not meant to be this way. Paul told us to 'carry each other's burdens' (Galatians 6:2). We are supposed to share our problems with each other. The rest of the verse says 'in this way you will fulfil the law of Christ'. Fulfil –

fill each other with the power of love. The law of Christ is the summation of all other laws governing human relationships; the law of Christ is found in Matthew 22:37–39. Christ said, "'Love the Lord your God with all your heart and with all your soul and with all your mind." This is the first and greatest commandment. And the second is like it: "Love your neighbour as yourself."' One of the ways to love our neighbour as ourself is to listen to each other's problems, to be understanding, and to attempt to help.

The Gospels resound with examples of Jesus' understanding of people. The Samaritan woman, Mary Magdalene and Zacchaeus all experienced the supreme understanding of the Master, and because he understood them, they felt his power, they received some of his power, their lives were transformed.

Forgiveness

There is a second part to good therapy (and a third). The first is being understood, as was just talked about; the second part is finding out why you did something, how it came about, why you feel the way you do. The third part is change, learning how to change.

In the act of hearing why, of coming to understand yourself, there is power. In this act of understanding yourself, you are often able to forgive yourself, and receiving forgiveness is one of the most power-filling events in anyone's life. Forgiveness is the antidote for guilt, and as I said in the last chapter, guilt is a power drainer.

No one could tell from the outside that Laura had a problem with guilt. She was one of those women who made heads turn when she entered a room. Not only did she have a flair for dressing in ways which flattered her figure, but she had what is called a presence. Her posture would have made a military squadron leader proud and she walked as if she owned the world, but at the same time, there was no sense of arrogance about her.

Laura's problem was her past. Even though she appeared so self-confident, Laura did not like herself very much. In therapy, going over Laura's upbringing and life as a young adult, it became obvious that she had never really felt loved, either by parents or in a relationship. She was about as power empty a person as I had ever known, yet she looked wonderful on the outside. As a teenager, Laura had sought love wherever she could get it. She craved the touching and affection she received from a boy and she had so little self-confidence that she always gave in to having sex, hoping this would make the boy like her more. She soon gained a reputation for being 'easy'. As she got older, she realised her 'easiness' had the opposite effect; she never had a boyfriend for long. So she had years ago stopped that self-destructive behaviour, but she still felt guilty about it, still believed within herself that her bad reputation was justified. Because of this, she was always choosing men who were inferior to her; unconsciously, she did not think she deserved anyone better.

When her problem was seen in the light of the *Powerdigm*, I was able to show Laura that she had simply been looking for love, trying to be filled up. Sex is often used as a temporary power filler; Laura's search for closeness with boyfriends by giving in to sex was never going to satisfy her heart's longings and her guilt had been a warning buzzer, trying to get her to stop.

I did not, however, tell Laura she should not feel guilty. When we have done something we should not have done, guilt is a God-given emotion meant to bring us to rectify a situation. In other words, the power draining which comes from feeling guilty is healthy; it is meant to make us think twice, to repent and to receive forgiveness. However, if we label ourselves as 'bad' rather than feeling bad about what we've done, the guilt can become crippling. And if we feel guilty about something we shouldn't feel guilty about, the emotion of guilt can be a life-waster, robbing us of ever attaining inner peace. That is why the feelings of guilt need to be talked about, need to be shared with one trusted person, so that they can be analysed and ultimately healed.

Guilt is not meant to be a permanent condition; it is merely a passage through which we go on our way to being forgiven, like a foyer of a house; we are not meant to stay there, but to go on into the living room. It is difficult to truly 'live' when we are power empty and guilt is a supreme power drainer.

Laura did not need forgiveness from others; she needed it from herself and ultimately, from God. She needed to forgive herself, to understand why she did what she did, to learn from that time in her life and to move on, to move from the foyer to the living room. It was not easy and it did not happen overnight; it was a process. As Laura began to understand why she did what she did, her image of herself slowly began to change and she was gradually able to forgive herself for her past.

Forgiveness, whether of ourselves or of others, is supremely power filling and forgiveness is not temporary; if genuine, it lasts. For many, the experience of being forgiven by God is often their entry into a relationship with him through Christ. The Bible tells us that God values a broken and contrite heart. Why? The answer, which can be attested to by anyone who has ever truly repented and come to know God in this manner, is that we need, actually need, God's forgiveness in order to be freed from guilt. I believe all psychological processes are God-given. We are set up that way, built that way.

A person such as Laura can benefit greatly from counselling that allows her to understand herself and ultimately
look back and forgive that young girl who was so desperate for love. But she, or anyone, would benefit much more
by receiving God's forgiveness. Jesus told the woman taken
in adultery to 'Go now and leave your life of sin' (John
8:11). He not only forgave her; he understood her and
loved her. Forgiveness is a power full thing.

Helping others

Everything I have described so far, these power fillers, are
great to have, to experience. Much better to have some
power-filling incidents than none or few. Unfortunately
though, many of them are temporary. After the sport or
skill is mastered, after the wardrobe is filled with new
clothes, after the new car is bought, are we happy? Yes, but
not for long. So what is permanent? As I've been saying all
through this book, love is the only permanent power filler.
Being loved and/or loving someone are the only permanent ways to become power full. Coming to know God
through Christ is the ultimate way to feel loved, to become
power full. That will be described in the final chapter of
this book. But we also need relationships on a human level.

What if one is alone? What if there is no one, no one who
reciprocates your love in terms of a spouse or a relationship? What if there is no family, or a dysfunctional family
– then what? There are many, many people these days in
our isolative, individualistic society who are all alone,
completely alone. Very often, these people turn inward and
become bitter, self-pitying and hence, power drained. This
is so sad, sad because it could be so different for them if
they would only reach out to others and in that reaching
out, be power filled.

Helping others is one way to become power full if there

is no one in a person's life. Missionaries, medical volunteers and those whose profession helps others all testify to the rewards, the good feelings they receive inside, when others are helped through them. Most of us have said at some time or another, 'I got a lot more out of it than I put in.' When we serve others, when we do something for other people, it makes us feel power full. The more we help others, the more we feel power full. I believe this is another of those laws of the universe I spoke of in the first chapter; it is not a law of physics, but it is just as certain. It is a law of power.

We all admire people like Albert Sweitzer and Mother Teresa. Their sacrifice, giving up what most of us seek in terms of material possessions and comforts, gave back to them in abundance what they relinquished. It is true that we need intimacy, one-to-one connections with people who can fill us with love. It is true that we need to be filled up, not just to fill. But it is circular. The more one loves, the more love one receives. The key to this means of becoming power full is in numbers. When good is done for others, plural, over and over again in many situations, most people will end up feeling power full.

And for those who are already power full, who do have inner peace, helping others adds to the power full feeling inside. A person who is power full has much power within, whether that person is alone in the world or loved by others. But if that person is able to give some of that power, in the form of love, to someone else, if someone else is able to receive it, then not only has the power become more visible, useful, but the person giving to others feels more complete.

Don Mroscak, of Los Angeles, California is the quintessential example of living to help others. For the past twenty-five years, as a counsellor at Garfield High School, he has been helping Latino students in East L.A., helping them to go on to college. Don, who is like a father to some, certainly a mentor to others, encourages them, inspires them, gives them confidence, helps win over reluctant parents, and many times helps them financially. Although he is now retired, he still goes to the school twice a week, continuing to help.

To many students, Mroscak has become a dad. To others, he is a friend, a protector and the ultimate mentor. His colleagues describe him as an innovator who works tirelessly with parents, teachers and the community to expand college opportunities for students. One of these colleagues, Ruby Solarzano, states, 'He truly is the most giving person I have ever met. He opens his home, his heart, his wallet for these kids', she says, then recites a litany of kindnesses he has shown students over the years, including giving money for college application fees and paying for air travel to college. Many times he has offered his home as shelter to kids who are kicked out of their homes and have no safe place to go.

Mr Mroscak grew up as the son of Polish immigrants who came to the United States in 1918. 'It is ironic, the similarities of the Mexican culture and the Polish culture,' he says. 'Basically, the majority of us are blue-collar workers; the majority of us are Catholic; and the majority of us keep to ourselves. We're afraid to go out of our neighbourhoods, our familiar surroundings.' This is why he encourages students to consider higher education and to venture beyond their communities when it comes to college.

Born in Springfield, Illinois, Don was brought up in the Midwest of the United States where he experienced prejudice, just as many Latinos do in Los Angeles. 'We were looked down on because we were Polish.' Don identifies with these kids; he knows what it was like growing up feeling different.

One of his students, Roy Torres, testifies to how selfless Don has been. 'I grew up on welfare. I came from a single-parent family with no father. Because Don believed in me, I began to believe in myself. He does what he believes and it works because it comes from his heart. He is the original good guy.'

Why does he do this? What does he get out of it? Don explains, 'What is important for me is the dream that I have, and that's to get youngsters here to realise that they should not be satisfied with just achieving average work but instead to go far beyond that. I tell my kids, "Don't wear blinders, don't think in square boxes, and don't take no for an answer. We've got to get Latino students in the college mainstream and let them know that they can have top-level jobs. We have to teach our young people to become leaders and then the leaders to become role models. We can't give up on our kids.'

As seen through the *Powerdigm* theory, what Don Mroscak is doing is filling these kids with power. He is instilling self-confidence in them, telling them they can do it, showing them ways for them to do it. He has, in a very real way, loved these kids, and not only has he given them love, but they have received it, they have come to believe him when he tells them they can do it; they have received the love and it has been a power-filling experience. A modest man, this counsellor doesn't like to talk about his accomplishments. 'It just seems to me I'm doing what everyone is supposed to do.' I agree with him, but how many of us do?

That's why Mroscak says he will continue to return to Garfield. 'We are all put on this earth for some reason. I was put here because I enjoy helping people more than anything else. I care about my kids. That's why I still come here,' he says. 'This is home.'[7]

Don Mroscak is to be envied. He has found his purpose in life and has learned the secret of happiness. Helping others has made him power full and at peace with himself.

CHAPTER 4

HOW WE ARE BUILT

When you build a house, you begin with a foundation. The framework is built upon the foundation and last of all come the details; the house gets completed, filled in, decorated, given certain touches that distinguish it from other houses. When you expound a theory, you begin the same way.

First the foundation. We all inherit certain predispositions, tendencies toward different psychological aspects of our personality. The foundation is our genetic make-up, our inherited tendencies. The framework is what happens after that, from the minute we were born, how we were brought up, how loving or knowledgeable about raising children our parents were, how functional or dysfunctional their lives were, our birth order in the family, our physical make-up, illnesses and/or accidents. All these things and many more create the framework of our personality. The details, the finishing touches, are analogous to our inner thinking, the way we look at the world. This is how the 'house' will look, either to ourselves or to others; this could be called our interior decorating.

The foundation

The foundation is fairly obvious. No one is surprised if a child turns out to look like one or both parents and this can be true of personality as well. It is easy to recognise the validity of the description 'chip off the old block'. When we are grown up and we catch ourselves saying something in the exact tone of voice of one of our parents, that moment when we hear ourselves use the same negative sounds we swore to ourselves we would never use, we usually blame ourselves for not following through on our promise (to ourselves) that we would never do that. It is only natural, however, because we probably inherited those tendencies, predispositions toward personality, like them or not.

There have been studies on twins who were brought up apart and never knew each other or their real parents, twins who were adopted at birth by separate sets of parents. Many things are alike about these twins, sometimes the way they walk, their food preferences, their choice of career. These things could not have been learned; these characteristics had to have been inherited. So a great deal of our personality arrived with us, even before we were born.

Framework

The framework correlates to the things we have learned all our lives by being around others in our family and our environment. The framework was built during our growing-up years. During those years we watched our parents act however they acted, for good or for bad. We watched and learned. We might not have liked how one or both parents acted; we may have vowed we would never do that, but we still learned it. We not only watched our parents, we watched our siblings, our friends, teachers, neighbours – everyone around us. Whether we were conscious of it or not, we were watching and learning.

Interior decorating

The inside of the house is our responsibility. We fill in the details. We can leave the house a mess or we can clean it up and make it beautiful. Some were given a beautiful house by their family, yet even those people can get sloppy and let things slide. Others were given a very ugly house and need to work extra hard to make it beautiful. It is good news to know that these details can be rearranged, cleaned up, made nicer; the way the house looks can be changed. Not without a lot of hard work, usually not without some pain, but we, our house, can change in the interior. However, if there are cracks in the foundation, if the framework was shaky at best, there is obviously structural repair to be done.

Poor foundation/framework

Janet was always referred to as 'a skinny little thing', even though she doesn't remember ever being hungry for food. What she does remember is a constant sense of loneliness, of being hungry for attention. With four brothers and two sisters and many cousins and aunts and uncles around, it wasn't that she was physically alone, but her mother was always busy or tired or gone, working three jobs to feed the family, and by the time Janet was old enough to remember, her father had left, never to be heard from again.

Somehow, she always lost out in getting what she wanted from the others in her family. When Janet was little, if she had a toy and it was taken away from her, she was never able to work out how to get it back. She wasn't a very good fighter and no one paid any attention to her when she cried, so most of the time she just gave up. As she grew older, and tensions increased in her large family, she would try to just go away, to hide somewhere, to be alone. She didn't like fighting; she wouldn't stand up for herself and no one had ever stood up for her, so she learned to cope by avoiding these situations.

She felt powerless to change anything. By the time she was a teenager, she had learned that if she was very quiet and very good and very helpful to others, she could, sometimes, get a small amount of recognition. Not much, not often, but a little bit. So Janet became a placator, a person who always has to please, a person who never gets what she wants, but at least keeps others from being angry at her.

By the time she was an adult, she had passed from just being a placator to being a manipulator. She manipulated people by doing so much for them that they felt beholden to her. She volunteered for every committee and job in her church; she was always doing 'good' for others, but behind the good deeds was the implicit message 'I do so much for you, you should like me, value me, ask me to your parties, vote me chairperson' – and many more such thoughts.

Janet would never have described herself this way. From her perspective, she was always misunderstood; she was the one trying to do the right thing and everyone else was mowing her down. If anyone had accused her of being a manipulator, she would have been shocked and hurt and would think that once again, no one understood her. What had evolved, unconsciously, was a way to gain a little bit of power.

Janet never felt in control, either of herself or of others in her family. She had no control over her father leaving and she had no control over her mother's seeming neglect. She also felt she had no control over her emotions; she was powerless, as children often are. So, as an adult, she was still being very quiet and very good, trying to earn love and attention. She got attention all right and she got some power, but it was mostly negative power. She was still struggling to be filled up.

Good foundation/framework

Jim grew up in very different circumstances. He was the long-awaited son of older parents. His parents had married late, in their mid-thirties; at least it was considered late in those days. Even though they wanted a child very badly, his mother did not conceive until they had been married several years. So the pregnancy and his arrival and everything surrounding those events was received joyously; his birth was celebrated.

Jim received plenty of attention and certainly never knew the feeling of loneliness, of emptiness that Janet felt. He was made to feel that he was wonderful; he was loved not only by his parents, but by two sets of doting grandparents. He was not spoiled; his parents were intelligent in their child rearing. He was brought up in a manner which created a very self-confident, trusting, kind adult, an adult who was able to give to others, give back the love that had been given to him.

Jim was filled with power; the power of being loved, the power of being paid attention to, the power of being told he was important to those surrounding him. He was socially secure in his world; he felt filled up. Jim knew he was loved and wanted, and, because of this, he had no need to struggle for anything. Nor did he easily understand those who did; he was power full.

Too much power?

Is there such a thing as being given too much power by our parents? Yes, because like too much of anything, it is not balanced. The self is esteemed to the neglect of others' feelings. If a child is made to feel so important that what he or she wants is always magically provided, if a child is never thwarted, is undisciplined, then when they go out into the world, go to school and on into adulthood, they may think the world is there for them alone, just as it was when they were a child. These people who were given too much power as children have problems as adults because they seem unaware of others' wants or needs.

However, in my experience, people who have been given too much power is not as big or as widespread a problem as the opposite. It is low self-esteem, lack of power, and insecurity which drives people at the other end of the continuum to abnormal behaviour. Other than biochemically caused mental illnesses, I believe this lack of love, lack of this positively charged power, is at the root of most emotional and psychological problems.

Foundation or framework?

In Jim's case, environmental factors appear to be the chief input into his growing up to be a happy, well-adjusted individual. He was given the power of love as a child and as he grew up, he had no need to struggle for other kinds of power. It appears that he was a very malleable child; he responded to his parents' intentions and did not rebel against them.

If he had been born angry, as some parents describe their difficult children, difficult even in the very beginning, he still could have turned out as he did, with only occasional temper flare-ups as evidence of his inherent personality. If there is not some biochemical imbalance leading to personality problems, then wise and caring child rearing can go a long way toward overcoming negative genetic predispositions.

In Janet's case, both genetic and environmental factors played a part. If she had been brought up by a family who filled her with love, with self-confidence, with power, she would not have become a placator, a manipulator. These natural tendencies which originate with a giving-up type of personality (remember the little girl who couldn't get her toys back) would have been there, but if someone had been able to carefully and lovingly teach little Janet how to get her toys back, if someone had got them back for her, then each of these scenarios would have resulted in a much different adult Janet.

Janet's inherent trait of being hurt rather than angry explains her behaviour. Hurt and anger are closely tied; this will be illustrated more fully in the chapter on anger. Janet was pretty much left to fend for herself and this is how she coped. Although it did not look as if she was struggling for power (since she appeared to give up), she actually was; by being manipulative she gained some measure of power. It was not satisfactory; she certainly did not feel full, but she was not quite as empty after she had obtained something she wanted. Given a different genetic make-up, she could have responded to her environment in more rewarding ways.

The way we cope is often simply an attempt to gain some power, to feel filled up. One of Janet's brothers, growing up in the very same family, could have and probably did react very differently to their circumstances. We can conjecture that he might have reacted very angrily. His nature might have been to fight for his rights and he may have continued fighting all his life. Whether he got into trouble for robbing a bank and went to prison or whether he became MD of a large company, the personality, the dynamic of looking out for himself first above all others, could have been identical. Also, his reactions could have been one of the reasons Janet reacted as she did.

When a teenager or any child, for that matter, rebels, is disobedient, he is gaining some power for himself. It is definitely a negative force, but it is power nevertheless. Does this have to happen? Why do some never rebel? Why do some children who have been brought up in very strict homes and/or strict religions rebel so strongly?

Answering these questions one at a time; no, it doesn't have to happen. There are no statistics on the number of children who do not rebel, who obey their parents, who appear to be so power full that rebellion is not necessary. When we see this happen, we tend to attribute it to the nature of the child. But remember, it is not only the foundation; the framework contributes greatly, the learning the child did in his home. Jim's case is a good example of someone who felt no need to rebel, no need to be filled with any kind of power; he was already power full. His parents appear to have been power full themselves, else they would not have been able to bring him up so well. The love bestowed on him, out of their reservoir of love, made him power full; therefore he had no need to try to gain power in other ways. He was content within himself.

This is the way things are supposed to be, but unfortunately, seldom are. Jim's case is presented as the ideal. Most of us as parents fall somewhere in between the example of Jim's parents and Janet's. If parents are not power full themselves, it is difficult to meet those ideal standards.

As to why children who have been raised in very strict homes, strict religions, often rebel, it is this same struggle for power, only exponentially. In other words, the more the lid has been put on us, the more we will struggle for freedom, for power. If, added to this, the strictness is abusive, either physically or emotionally, rather than done with love, then the need to gain control will be even greater.

Being an adolescent is often a continuous struggle for power. No longer children, adolescents struggle against the power of their parents or any authority. As children, they are powerless; but as adolescents they want to begin making decisions for themselves; they resist being restrained. They rebel and in that rebellious act there is a sense of being filled with power. The more powerless they feel, the more they will struggle for power.

Parents

So far the focus has been on the children; what about the parents? What kind of parents are able to bring up the best children? By best, I mean the children who grow up like Jim, like Maria, those who feel power full, have an inner peace, therefore are happy.

Men who come into therapy often have deep-rooted problems with their fathers; women often have similar problems with their mothers.

A father who has been extremely successful in his career can be very hard for a son to live up to. If a man's father is very successful, appears to 'do everything right', the son may feel like a failure unless his track record is similar. His father's power can be a power drainer for him. Rather than place himself on the continuum of power in relation to his father, the son may come to believe he is powerless, not only in comparison to his father, but in all relationships, when in actuality he may not be. Whether the son feels this way or not depends upon how his father treats his own success, as well as how he treats the son. Obviously, if the success is what is most important to the father, he is going to pass on that message to his son, either overtly or covertly. However, if the father is truly power full, filled with positive power, and is successful as well, then there will be no adverse reactions in the son.

What about the opposite? What about a weak father? If a father is weak, seemingly powerless, this can also have negative ramifications on the son. It can either be a springboard for determination to be different from the father, by overcompensating and becoming obnoxiously powerful, or a son can blame his powerlessness on his father and not try. One thing is certain – a weak father is unable to give the son what he needs as a child. Not power full himself, he is unable to fill that child with the kind of power he needs.

How do these fathers affect their daughters? Unlike sons, a powerful father is not someone a daughter needs to compete with. She will probably admire him greatly, perhaps worship him, even if he is physically absent from home a great deal and/or emotionally absent. The negative results from a powerful father often do not manifest themselves in a daughter until she is grown up and married or grown up and seeking males who live up to her image of her father, usually a difficult task. Men may constantly disappoint her as she searches for the perfect (idealised) father as a mate.

A powerless father is also a detriment to a daughter because his powerlessness may have created a powerful mother or perhaps it was the other way around; a very powerful mother may have created the dynamic of a powerless father. In these cases, daughters often 'catch' their mother's contempt for their father, which will also have an impact on their relationships with men as an adult.

Men may be seen as weak, making it more difficult for these daughters to establish egalitarian, balanced relationships.

Mothers who are powerful in a negative sense of the word are very destructive to both genders. The son grows up with a fear of women, often a deep, underlying hatred of them. The daughter is affected just as was the son with a powerful father; she will feel powerless under the influence of her strong mother. A weak, powerless mother could bring out nurturing qualities in a daughter, but often the role model replicates in the next generation and another powerless woman brings up children who then mimic her.

Again, the balance of power is relevant. If one or both parents are powerful in a negative manner (rather than power full in a positive manner) or if one or both parents are power empty, this will impact the way their children are brought up. The best parents are those who have no need to engage in power struggles either with each other or with their children. Seen in the light of the *Powerdigm*, parenting is often a day by day, year by year struggle for power – either between the parents for control of the child or between the parents and the children, or both. The best parents are power full.

These parent-child relationships just given are very generalised and exceptions always abound. In all instances, both genetic and learning aspects are present.

The good news is that anyone, at any point in his or her life, can change, can break this pattern; we are not doomed either by our genes or our histories. It is not always possible to understand whether our inherited personality traits were learned or whether we were born with them. Being genetic does not mean it cannot be changed, but it does explain the source. Those traits you know you learned are even easier to change; unlearning is possible.

So this is how we are built. There is another very important part of our foundation that hasn't been discussed – whether we were born male or female. That story comes next.

CHAPTER 5

GIRLS AND BOYS – WHAT A DIFFERENCE!

Julia went to work straight out of an MBA course for a managed health care firm. She started at a good salary and was thrilled to be on her way in the corporate world. Over a five-year period, she moved up into more and more responsible positions, gaining authority and increasing her earnings. As a single woman, one who was bright and attractive, she was in several relationships before meeting John, the man she ultimately married.

John was an insurance agent when they first met and was as successful as Julia. However, within a year after their marriage, a recession hit the nation and along with it, John's success in selling new insurance policies. At first, neither of them was worried. Julia certainly made enough to support them and they were sure things would pick up again. But the economy only got worse and as John met with rejection after rejection, he grew more anxious and then finally depressed. It seemed to Julia that the man she had married no longer existed; he was quiet and moody. When she came home from work and had something interesting or exciting to tell him, he didn't react the way he had previously. In his mind, not in hers, he was not only failing; he was a failure.

John and Julia were fairly equal in terms of power when they met. While John was still successful, he was very proud of Julia's success; he boasted about her to his friends and did nothing but encourage her as she continued to move up the corporate ladder. However, as John's earning ability plummeted, the equation changed; the balance of power shifted. On the power continuum, in relationship to Julia, he saw himself as less powerful, one down. Julia did not feel more powerful than John; she felt just the same as she had before. As John struggled for what he perceived as a lack of power, their relationship suffered.

John began struggling for power by finding fault with almost everything Julia did. Unconsciously, he was trying to regain the position of equality that had been there before. If he showed himself to be 'right' about any topic or action of hers, he had gained some power. It was negative power, but in a twisted sort of way, it made him feel a little better.

What would have happened if he had been single and the same events occurred in his career? Or what if he had been married to someone who wasn't as successful as Julia was in her job? My conjecture is that he would have been upset, maybe even depressed, but it was all made worse because of his self-perceived position in relation to Julia.

How it all started

Men and women react to power with distinct differences. Some of these differences can be traced to inborn traits that we were given for the survival of the species. Some are due to innate, individual personality traits and many more can be attributed to all the events which ended up shaping the framework of our lives.

In spite of men's greater sensitivity today, and awareness of their need to be more involved in their children's lives than their fathers were in theirs, few people would disagree that, in general, most women have stronger nurturing instincts than do men, nurturing instincts which are directed toward their children and their husbands and in some cases, out into society.

These instincts were very necessary at the beginning of civilisation. Someone had to stay home and take care of the children or the race would not have survived. Why women did this rather than men was due to the simple fact that women carried food for the child in her body, a talent men did not have. Conversely, most would agree that men and boys display more aggression, more combativeness (at least physically) than do women. This again was adaptive. Someone had to go out and hunt the bear, kill it, bring it home to the hearth. Physically, males are built for this chore to a more highly developed level than are women.

In the twentieth century, these roles gradually faded away so that now it is perfectly possible for a woman to support the household (that is, kill the bear) and a man is completely capable of feeding the child (with milk in a bottle). However, just as we have appendixes that are no longer necessary, we also have some of the personality tendencies, some of the emotions, which were adaptive in the beginning of civilisation.

What does God have to say about this balance of power between men and women? This is a controversial subject, but very relevant to the theme of this book. I will explore one of the more familiar passages and then give my own opinion, with the qualifying statement that it is just that – my opinion!

Biblical principles

Submit to one another out of reverence for Christ. Wives, submit to your husbands as to the Lord. For the husband is the head of the wife as Christ is the head of the church, his body, of which he is the Saviour. Now as the church submits to Christ, so also wives should submit to their husbands in everything. Husbands, love your wives, just as Christ loved the church and gave himself up for her to make her holy, cleansing her by the washing with water through the word, and to present her to himself as a radiant church, without stain or wrinkle or any other blemish, but holy and blameless. In this same way, husbands ought to love their wives as their own bodies. He who loves his wife loves himself. After all, no one ever hated his own body, but he feeds and cares for it, just as Christ does the church – for we are members of his body. For this reason a man will leave his father and mother and be united to his wife, and the two will become one flesh. This is a profound mystery – but I am talking about Christ and the church. However, each one of you also must love his wife as he loves himself, and the wife must respect her husband.

(Ephesians 5:21–33)

What does the word 'submit' mean? It does not mean that a wife should submit to physical abuse; it does not mean that a wife should submit to verbal abuse, and it must be set into the context of the entire passage.

The notes in the NIV state that the word 'submit' in these verses is an aspect of the mutual submission taught in the beginning of this passage. To submit meant to yield one's own rights. If the relationship called for it, as in the military, the term could connote obedience, but that meaning is not called for here. In fact, the word 'obey' does not appear in Scripture with respect to wives, though it does with respect to children and slaves. These notes go on to say that a woman ought to submit to her husband as an act of submission to the Lord.[8]

We rail against the word 'submit' because it has connotations of control, of domination; it can even be interpreted sexually. A power-empty man who goes to church and reads these verses could very well misuse them, conveniently not seeing the rest of the verses which instruct the husband to love his wife. If a power-empty person naturally struggles for power, then the word 'submit' can be used in a way that I am sure God would not sanction.

The key to all this is that a man is supposed to be honourable. None of us have a problem giving honour to Christ, because he is honourable. When a man treats his wife as these verses demand, loving her as much as he loves himself, then I believe a woman innately wants to honour him. As Christians, if we believe we are created by God, which means created with all our gender differences, hormonally as well as physically, and if we read and accept Scripture, then we have to hearken back to these difficult verses quoted above.

There is much in them we can learn about marriage, much for husbands to learn as well as wives. *Promise Keepers*, an organisation that ministers to men, has a list of seven promises that men are to keep. When these promises are kept, it is my belief that women want to honour their husbands, which will make a man feel more power full, which will make him love his wife more, which will bring her to a willingness to submit to her husband (however she interprets that word). When a husband does not keep his marriage vows, his promises, when a man does not love his wife as he does himself, then the contract in these verses is broken. A wife should not submit to a man who does not keep his part of the bargain.

I believe most women do seek a man who is somewhat higher on the power continuum than she is, consciously or not. Women do not like to look down on a man; most women do not like to be in control of a man, even if they struggle to do so. I believe these passages are meant to reflect the ideal of what marriage should be. The problem is, it is difficult for a woman to feel submissive to someone she feels is her inferior and I am speaking in all contexts when I say this. I believe a Christian woman wants her husband to be the spiritual leader in the home, if anything, ahead of her in spiritual matters. She wants someone who is wise and learned, who does not treat her as his inferior, but rather who leads the way spiritually in their home.

I also believe this is true in the secular world. Psychologically speaking, I believe women instinctively search for someone whom they can look up to, respect. They want to take care of a man in a nurturing way, but they do not want to support him, ward off the dragons for him; they want him to be strong and do this for himself. Most women do not want to be more powerful in a relationship; they either want equality or they want to be right next to their man on the power continuum, with him higher. Higher, not in the sense of control over her, but higher in that she looks 'up' to him.

Men hold; women are held. The embrace can be seen as a metaphor for a relationship. Of course, there are times when a man likes to be held and times when a woman likes to hold, but most of the time, it is more natural the other way. In this embrace, a woman feels secure, powerful, because she feels loved, while the man feels powerful because he is loving someone.

It should also be mentioned that these verses in Scripture are about husband-wife relationships; they say nothing about men and women in other contexts. In other words, there is no injunction for women to be naturally lower on the power continuum in the world of work or in any other relationship than the marital one.

After wrestling with these verses for years, after being very rebellious against them (and at times against Paul!), I have made my peace with them. I do believe this is the ideal, that is the way we are 'built'. Yet I still think these verses can be abused by men who do not feel power full and take it out on someone they see as much lower on the power continuum than are they.

Male power

Little boys learn very early that they have to be strong. The strongest one wins in interaction with each other. Boys not only need to be strong to stand up to the bully in the playground, they also have their manhood tested constantly in terms of athletic ability and the little guy who is scared or unable to defend himself, who doesn't even like to roughhouse, feels powerless. If he is fortunate, he is made to feel power full for other reasons at home, but far too often his parents say, 'You have to learn to be a man!'

Because of this, I maintain that men are more aware of a need for power than are women. This is simply because of the role given them in society, also dating back to when they had to kill the bear. When the woman stayed home to tend the hearth and feed the child, it is doubtful she got any rave reviews for her job, but when the men came in from a hunt, everyone celebrated. A man who did not deliver the goods was looked down on by all and that was dangerous, because then another man could, would dare to, move in and take away his woman.

So we are left with an archaic legacy in which many men appear to need to feel powerful around women. That is why there is chauvinism on the job, in the corporate world. It is not that men really do not believe a woman can do the job; it is that if a woman can do the job just as well, what does that say about his power?

Strength

An obvious difference in males and females is physical strength. Physical strength is a clear-cut example of power. I have always wondered what would happen if women were the stronger sex physically. If all or most men were smaller than women, if we knew that they could not hit back, would we women be just as violent? Would there be more battered men? Historically, more crimes have been committed by men than women. Again, I would attribute this to physical strength. I do not believe men are more evil or less moral than women; more crimes are committed by men simply because they have the power to do it; they commit more crimes because they can.

Men also hold more power positions in the world than women simply because they can. Women try to control to gain power, men just control. Men began in control because of their superior strength physically and the world has basically remained that way. If women fought all the wars, with only back-up support from men, if women had started off killing the bear and all the men and the women in the world expected them to be the leaders, then the balance of power would have been different.

Money

A man who is power full, secure, is not threatened by a wife who may earn more money than he does or by a woman who is his boss; this man will be able to accept, unemotionally, these states. He does not need to feel one up with the woman in his life; he does not have to need to prove himself, but he does not want to feel one down either.

Women bristle at inequalities in society in terms of laws and job opportunities, as they should. The fight women have had to wage to gain equal pay for equal work, which is still a long way from occurring, is a hangover from the days when men were expected to kill the bear. It is ironic to me when I hear of a woman in a divorce settlement situation feeling outraged that a man would expect alimony from her if she is the top earner. Some of this is justified, since because of the double standard in earnings, she feels he has more chance to support himself in the long term than she does. However, this is a sign that women still feel, at some level, that he should be out killing the bear. In other words, women want it both ways; we are in a transition period.

*   *   *

This chapter began by telling the story of a couple who had begun their relationship on an equal level in terms of power. We left John feeling powerless and inferior to Julia and Julia feeling frustrated. Their story will be picked up in the next chapter, on relationships.

CHAPTER 6

ROMANTIC RELATIONSHIPS – WHO HAS THE POWER?

There are many kinds of relationships – romantic, work, family, friends, customer, landlord – the list could go on and on. This entire book is about power in relationships; this chapter will deal specifically with romantic relationships.

Romantic relationships are the easiest of all situations in which to learn about power. In this arena, one person has more power than the other one. It may not be the same person who has more power; the positions may change; they may even change frequently, but seldom are both people equal in power. The reason one person has more power than the other is that the person who cares the most is in a one-down position.

The story of John and Julia was told in the last chapter. When John moved himself down on the continuum of power in relation to Julia, he had at first struggled for negative power, by being moody, by contradicting whatever she said. Julia couldn't cheer him up; nothing she tried to do mattered; he was still despondent. If she spent any money on herself or on things for their home, he either overtly objected, or she was met with an icy look. Soon everything about their relationship changed, even their sexual life. John didn't appear interested in sex any more and Julia felt hurt, rejected. She was not a saint; after trying to deal with his depression as if it was just a momentary phase, she grew disillusioned and began to wonder if she had married the wrong man.

When she stopped trying to cheer him up, when she gave up trying to change the way he was thinking about himself, she withdrew emotionally. When Julia did that, John felt desperate to retain, even regain Julia's love. He realised she was reacting to him more coolly than before; that was one of the reasons he felt less powerful around her. His interpretation of how Julia felt about him was correct. Because their relationship was no longer equal, John began striving to please her; he was put back in the courting stage that made it seem to him that he cared more for Julia than she did for him. Because of this, she now had the most power in the relationship.

Julia still loved John, but she no longer felt 'in love'. What is the difference between being in love and loving someone? First, I want to define the concept of love using the metaphor of power.

Power of love

There is no stronger power than the power of love. Being loved has the power to change us, literally transform us. Think of power as an energy; it flows, as does electricity. When we are in love, we are in an altered state; being in love is a feeling caused by the excessive amount of power charging through us. We are absolutely overflowing with this power, this energy. It is a state of euphoria; the power is in full force, filling, consuming us. That is why it feels so good; our cup is so full it is bursting. We are never more power full than when we are in love and that love is being returned.

When two people are equally in love, they have relinquished their power to each other. What does this mean? If I am in love with someone, he has power over me, simply because I'm in love with him. They say love is blind, and it is. I will excuse his behaviour to myself, rationalise, and 'let him get away with murder'. I have relinquished my own internal power to him. And he to me. This puts both of us in a very vulnerable position and each of us must trust to the good will of the other.

However, when there is inequality, the one who is less in love has most of the power, will be in a one-up position, has much less to lose. Why? Because the person who is loved more cannot get hurt or at least cannot get hurt to the same degree that the person who is unsure of the love can. This vulnerability to get hurt is a power drainer. When there is inequality in a relationship, one person is always striving to be filled up and one person feels filled up and therefore is not striving. This can be perceived as being emotionally distant by the one who is anxious, worried.

We are attracted to people and fall in love for all kinds of reasons, some of them not so grand. If we are power empty, we probably fall in love with anyone who acts even partly interested in us. We need the power of love so much that we will take it from any quarter, whether it is an appropriate person or not. 'Women who love too much' was a popular phrase a few years ago. I do not believe anyone can love too much, but we can be so hungry for the power of love that we will take anything we can get, settle for any amount of love, however small it is. This can be interpreted as loving too much. A person who is power full will be much less likely to take up with just anybody; he or she will be more discriminating.

Being in love

Being in love is very much like being in a constant state of anxiety. It is the ultimate rush. If both people are equally in love, this anxiety is experienced as pleasurable. If we are loved by someone we are in love with, there is a balance of power; we both feel equally filled up, power full. The act of loving someone, as opposed to 'being in love' is also a power filler, but it is a steady, constant source of power as opposed to the rush of new love.

Anxiety is also an emotion we may feel when we love someone and we are unsure of how he or she feels about us, but this type of anxiety can be agonising rather than pleasurable. We are fearful; this anxiety keeps us focused on that person, searching every event, every conversation, every look for confirmation that the same degree of interest exists in him or her. Or perhaps the relationship was balanced in the beginning, in terms of our interest being reciprocated, but then the other person withdraws, begins acting coolly. Anxiety sets in.

Often this anxiety we feel is interpreted as being in love, when actually it could be nothing but fear of losing the other one. Fear is anxiety and many people fear, dread being alone. Added to that may be the typical preoccupation with the person, which may be just that – preoccupation, but which can be interpreted as love. In many ways it feels the same. We tell ourselves that if it wasn't love, we wouldn't care so much what the other person did or did not do; we wouldn't be so obsessed. We may label this anxiety as 'being in love'.

Alan met Sandy at a party for single people. He had been attending these parties for over a year, hoping to meet someone new since his wife had filed for divorce. Alan had not wanted to divorce; he liked being married and he was not that dissatisfied with the marriage, but like it or not, he found himself divorced, alone, and lonely. He was not the type of person who coped well on his own. He could take care of himself, but he wanted someone to share things with, to go out to places with, eventually to marry. When he met Sandy, he was very impressed by her outgoing personality and her friendliness. She seemed to like him and he asked her if he could phone.

When he got home from the party that night, he felt wonderful. Sandy had given him her phone number, why not just ring right now? So he did. Sandy was surprised, but she was cordial and they arranged to meet a few nights later. Alan could hardly wait; that's all he thought about.

They met in a small, intimate restaurant downtown, dimly lit, with mahogany furnishings and tiled floors. Alan's first impressions of Sandy were reinforced. The way she smiled, the way she shook her short blonde hair when she laughed, and the fact that she seemed genuinely interested in what he was saying, all these added up to a sense of giddiness in Alan. It seemed to him they really hit it off; they seemed to have so much in common. 'I really felt I was falling in love,' Alan remembers.

He began phoning Sandy every night after work. Sometimes she wasn't home and he would leave a message. Then he would worry, obsessed about where she was and who she was with. He would phone her first thing the next morning, trying to appear casual, but trying to not so subtly find out where she had been.

Sandy began making excuses about not being able to see him. She suddenly was very busy, she said, and she really did not think she was ready for such an intense relationship right then. Alan was devastated. He constantly thought about everything he had said and done; 'What did I do wrong?' he questioned himself. 'Maybe I shouldn't have phoned so often. Maybe I should have acted more aloof.' Alan was miserable. He could not imagine that he wasn't in love with Sandy. Why else would he be thinking about her all the time?

It seemed to me that Alan was not in love. He was in heavy attraction, heavy interest, probably heavy lust, but not in love. He wanted Sandy to be just as interested in him as he was in her. When it became obvious that she was not, what Alan was experiencing was anxiety. He was also experiencing anger; he felt Sandy was mistreating him. From his point of view, she had acted just as interested in him as he was in her. Was she playing games? If so, Alan didn't like the rules.

Often when someone withdraws from us we vacillate between longing for that person to contact us, come back, and anger at them for treating us this way. 'How could she treat me like that! She must be a terrible person!' She may or may not be a terrible person; neither I nor Alan really knew enough about Sandy to make any judgements, but what I could tell from Alan's story was that Sandy was not as interested in him as he was in her and therefore she had much more power in the relationship. She was not striving to be filled up by him as he was by her. Therefore she could withdraw from this embryonic relationship with no anxiety (which is interpreted by the one who is left as 'being a terrible person').

Being in love vs. love

Unfortunately, the feeling of being in love is, as a rule, a temporary situation. If we fall in love it is usually at the beginning of a relationship. When that feeling doesn't last, when it goes away, we often interpret it as falling out of love. Why does that feeling go away? Why is it so temporary?

As reality sets in and we get to know each other on a moment-by-moment basis, with all our little idiosyncrasies and cross moods and imperfections, this interrupts the flow of power – this delicious energy which we had been experiencing. We chip away at the euphoria. We do not do it deliberately, but it usually happens nevertheless. Chinks appear in the pink cloud that has been enveloping us as we begin to build different assumptions about this wonderful person. There may still be ninety-eight characteristics about him or her that we love, but the four or five negative things we have begun to discover appear large; we think about them, brood over them, and probably, most of the time, enlarge them.

'I didn't know he had a temper,' you say to yourself, as if you didn't have a temper'. 'Well, I don't know if I can put up with that. So I had better set about trying to change him.' In the process of trying to change him, he resists, fights back, an argument ensues. 'Well, now I know lots more negative things about him, don't I? He argues! And he won't take my good and well-meaning advice! If he won't take my advice, that means I have no power over him. If I have no power over him, that means I am powerless. If I am powerless, then I had better start struggling for power here.' And so it spirals upward or downward, and pretty soon there are ninety-eight negative characteristics for each side to dwell on, since the negative characteristics are all either one is displaying.

All feelings are a direct result of our thoughts. Being in love causes all those wonderful feelings because consciously or unconsciously, we seek all our lives for the perfect match, the perfect love object. In the beginning of a relationship, we are sure we have found it. That is such an overwhelming thought that it causes overwhelming feelings. In the beginning of a relationship all our fantasies have come true. We idealise the person and think he or she is perfect. If they are perfect and they love me, then I must be pretty special too, or at least they make me feel special, and therefore all my scenarios for a perfect life are going to come true. No wonder we feel good at those times; we are made to feel good because we are being loved. Our cup is finally filled; filled with the power of love.

Three stages

There are three stages to a relationship. The first, we just talked about, the euphoric, being-in-love stage. Then as reality sets in and we begin to experience each other's faults, the stage of negotiating whether we are going to stay with this person begins. If a couple makes it through the second stage and work out their difficulties, then a third stage of ever-growing, deeper, companionable love begins.

And that is the answer to the question, that is the difference between loving someone and being in love. Loving someone is the result of a successful negotiating stage, the power balance is returned. Both people are equal in power. This is what successful marriage counselling does: gets couples through the negotiating phase and back to equality in power. If there is equality in power, then the feelings of being in love can reappear, be re-experienced from time to time while underneath flows a strong, steady current of power-full love.

Some couples marry or move in with each other in the first stage. When they try to work out their differences and cannot, the relationship ends. Others do not try to work out their differences and simply say that they do not love each other any more, with the same result – the relationship ends. Others stay together and never work out their differences, but quarrel all their lives and eventually live a joyless existence. However, if a couple stay together through the negotiating stage, which can last many years, and during those years do work things out, they will settle into the third stage of comfortable, companionable love. The rewards are worth it. Far too many people opt out too early, decide they have made a bad choice and move on. The problem is that the next relationship will present the same three stages, so unless someone wants to have serial relationships all his or her life, or end up alone, the negotiating needs to occur somewhere along the line.

Inequality

Christie certainly felt she had found her Prince Charming when she met Dave. He was good-looking, fun, and seemed to have all the qualities she felt she did not have. He had a graduate degree; Christie had never gone to college and didn't think she was clever enough to go anyway, but Dave didn't care about that at all! He told her that education had nothing to do with intelligence; he thought she was very bright and she did feel more clever around him.

Dave had an ordinary family. Christie defined ordinary as stable. His parents had not divorced; his parents were not alcoholics, as Christie's father was. His parents own a home and had saved to send Dave and his brothers to college. Now they were retired and played golf. Ordinary, middle-class folks with ordinary middle-class values.

This was very different from Christie's family. Her dad never kept a job very long; they had moved often. Finances always seemed precarious and all she heard she was supposed to do after high school was work more hours than she already did, 'so maybe you can help out a little'. These words, 'help out a little', were always said with sarcasm. So that's what Christie did; she got a job in a doctor's office as a secretary and she continued to work at night at her waitressing job, always feeling a little guilty that she didn't 'help out more'.

However, Dave took her to restaurants where someone else waited on her, he seemed to accept her just as she was. For the first time in her life, she didn't feel she was not measuring up to someone's expectations. It was such a relief.

Christie and Dave had fallen in love quickly; there was an immense physical attraction between them; their relationship was filled with passion. But after a few months, when the euphoria was beginning to fade, Christie began to realise that Dave was not perfect after all; he did have some faults. She was disillusioned; she had put him on a pedestal and now he seemed to come down a step or two every day. Dave was not disappointed in Christie; he was able to move successfully into the second phase of their relationship. But Christie was having a terrible time accepting Dave as he was when the haze of the being-in-love stage was over and their relationship began to be stormy. It was then that they came into therapy.

Christie was so power empty and being in love was so wonderful that she believed this was the answer to all her self-esteem issues. She was right; being loved by someone over a long period of time can be the answer. If one person stays with a power-empty person over a long, long time, that can be the means for the other to become power full and to believe in herself or himself. But instead, what often happens is the person who is trying to fill up the power-empty person becomes tired of trying and goes away. Then the power-empty one tells himself or herself they were right all along. Right, with a variety of reasons: 'I'm not worthy', or 'Men can't be trusted', or 'Mother was right'.

Christie and Dave are still in process; still trying to work out their differences. I have high hopes for them. My job is to restore the power balance. Dave loves Christie very much and is not, at this point, interested in changing partners, in looking for an easier, more equitable relationship. His love for her is healthy; he is not trying to get her to fill him up; that happened to him as a child. But Christie is in the one-down position because she needs Dave more than he needs her. When and if Christie can feel power full through therapy, and/or through his hanging in there and being stable for her, the power balance will be restored. She will not be in a one-down position and they will be able to go on to the third stage of a deep, companionable love.

At this point, the logical question to ask would be: What about God's love? Would not that solve all Christie's problems? If she came to know God through Christ and experienced the power of God's love, would not that be easier than going through therapy?

The answer is that of course, this is the ultimate answer for anyone. Christie would feel really power full for the first time in her life if she experienced God's love. But she still needs the love of another human being and she also needs to come to understand why she struggles for power so. Everyone is not going to be converted, just as everyone is not going to go to therapy. As a psychologist, I ask clients about their spiritual life, even when they have not brought up anything that would let me know they are involved in any type of faith, but everyone is not open to conversion. If I, as a psychologist, tell someone, 'All you need is Jesus Christ,' it would be similar to a Christian doctor telling a patient they should go and seek Christ's healing, rather than treat that patient with remedies that the doctor knows would benefit the patient.

Defences

Some people who have been hurt in the past, even if they are not power empty, will put up a defence and will not let themselves become vulnerable; they guard their power with all their might. What is a defence? It is a wall; a defence mechanism is like a wall that was built in childhood for protection from hurt. Repression is a defence mechanism; denial, over-compensation, these are just a few of the defence mechanisms. Building a wall, building a defence, is another way to say building power for oneself. It is a very effective, God-given way for us to cope as children when we are powerless. The wall was protective then, protective when the child was small and defenceless against the world, but just like Janet's habit of being a placator, this wall often remains as an adult when the circumstances no longer warrant it. In Christie's case and others like her, a steady, strong love over a long period of time will melt this defence, but the partner must have immense patience and have such a good internal sense of esteem that he or she can wait it out.

Inability to commit

Another common relationship problem is the man (or woman) who loses interest the minute he 'has' the other person. This is a familiar complaint, not only from those who have been in a relationship with these kind of people, but from those kind of people themselves. I remember particularly one thirty-five-year-old man who came to me with this history.

Gary was a plumber; his union paid for counselling and when a friend of his had received help with his marriage through marital therapy, Gary decided to 'come and see if you can answer some questions for me'.

His questions were about why he always lost interest in any young woman he had been seeing as soon as he did not have to pursue her. 'I just lose interest in a woman as soon as I know she is serious about me,' he told me. Gary smiled, nervously. 'I really want to get married, to have a home and children, but the same thing happens over and over again. I meet someone and we seem to hit it off and after a few months, I slowly begin to find fault with her. It seems as if the only type of woman I am interested in is someone I can't get! Why do I do this?'

Why? There was that question again, the one I hear over and over in therapy. There is never any simple answer to this question; the whys stem from many sources in every case, but putting Gary's problem into the *Powerdigm* theory gives a nice framework to the problem. 'Perhaps it is because you are afraid of losing your position of power,' I answered. 'What?' he was stunned. 'No,' he protested, 'I'm not in control when I can't get someone. Someone who won't pay any attention to me has the power, not me!'

I went on to explain to Gary that he and others like him who lose interest when someone is available for commitment are afraid of losing power. After years of hearing this complaint, I have reached the conclusion that not only Gary, but many others do this because of a fear of loss of control. As long as they are in pursuit, they are in control. When someone wants to commit themselves to them, there is an unconscious fear that their power will be diminished. This sounds backwards. It sounds as if they are out of control if they are chasing someone, but they aren't. It is true that Gary is not in control of the other person, but he is in control of himself, of his own power. So the minute someone is truly interested in him, he flees. If he commits himself to a relationship, he will become vulnerable; the woman will be able to hurt him if she withdraws from the relationship.

Observers of people like Gary might say he had an addiction, that he had to keep experiencing the thrill of a new conquest and could not stop himself. I believe that is just labelling the problem and does not help to solve it. Gary needed to work on his fear of becoming vulnerable; that was the ultimate solution.

Gary gave every appearance of someone who was power full. Good looking, in a roguish sort of way, he was like some of the leaves on my tree; he looked very good on the outside. He was not power empty, like Christie. He was somewhere along the continuum between power full and power empty, but he was not power full enough to risk becoming vulnerable; he kept a tight rein on his emotions.

Gary was different from those who are power empty because someone who feels no confidence in himself will only try for someone 'safe', a sure bet, or at the extreme, won't seek anyone at all, but will wait until someone comes to him. A totally powerless person is used to being one down, constantly out of control, and does not know how to be otherwise. A power-empty person will often give control, power, to others in a relationship simply because that is all he knows how to do. If the other person insists on not being the more powerful one, this may be too scary; he may not have respect for her any more and choose to leave.

What an impossible situation! How can anyone get out of this hopeless merry-go-round? The answer is: by staying in a situation long enough to work it through; by not looking for excuses to get out, by doing what is very, very hard, which is to change. Change, as well as become used to, adapt to, a new situation, a new power situation, a new power balance.

A good illustration of this was the conclusion to John and Julia's story. Good news on this one; Julia did hang in there. She really loved John and because she was not power empty, she was able to stick it out with him through the bad times. As they both began to understand about power and power struggles and balances of power, John's insecurity in the relationship lessened and his behaviour gradually changed. Fortunately, the economy began to change too, but the power balance had returned before that. They are now on a much stronger foundation. Why? Largely because they now know why.

CHAPTER 7

ADDICTIONS

Addictions are not only inner struggles, they are very serious. I am not going to address any of these problems in detail; each deserves its own book. I am simply going to show how they relate to the *Powerdigm*.

Addictions of food

There are three generally agreed-upon eating disorders: anorexia, bulimia and overeating. All three can be looked at through the eyes of the *Powerdigm*. Overeating is more common than the other two and all three can be life threatening. The word 'control' is often used in connection with food. Lack of control means being powerless and control means having power. In the case of anorexia, control itself is the comforter.

If someone is power empty or almost power empty, food can be a great comforter and for most of us in affluent societies, food can be an inner struggle.

Overeating

Helen had never had a problem with weight. She could eat all she wanted and seemed to stay at about eight stone. She bought good clothes and had some in her wardrobe that were quite a few years old. Everything still fitted.

But as Helen's career as a chemist grew, so did Helen. She began working more and more hours to salt away extra money for her wedding. After the wedding, she wanted to buy things for the house. Working long hours became a way of life for her. Since her husband was a doctor who was still a houseman at the hospital and was away from home for many hours day and night, she thought she might as well work. So even though she was working hard, not sitting around watching soap operas, she no longer had time for tennis three times a week; she was lucky to play once every two weeks. She gradually gave up jogging early in the morning; she was just too tired. She also began to eat a lot of junk food. Soon, much of Helen's wardrobe did not fit.

She wasn't too upset; everyone knows it is natural to put on a few pounds as you mature, and she needed new clothes anyway. What happened to Helen happens to many of us, she gained about three pounds a year. Helen's career was not all that was growing.

So Helen began to diet. As she began to diet, she began to realise how hard it was for her; she began to realise she was letting food rule her life. 'Here I am, an intelligent woman, who lets food draw me as if it had some innate power. That's ridiculous!' It is ridiculous, when we put eating into that framework. It is ridiculous for food to be so powerful and for a human being to be powerless around it, but we human beings do a lot of ridiculous things and most people, at least at some time in their lives, have a problem with food. Only when someone wants to lose weight more than he or she wants to overeat, will the weight loss occur.

How often have you heard someone say, 'I lost control, I

just had to eat that –', or, 'I simply can't control myself, I see a piece of chocolate cake and I just 'have to have it.' This is the inner struggle. If you overeat, it is because food controls you; you do not control food. Overeaters Anonymous recognises that concept in the first step of their Twelve Step programme which begins with the admission, 'I am powerless over food.' Admitting our powerlessness is the beginning of regaining power. We are sympathetic when someone has a problem stopping drinking or smoking or using drugs, because we know that these substances are addicting, that something physiological happens in our bodies to make us addicted. We are not sympathetic with ourselves or others when it comes to food addictions. Yet if we overeat, if we are overweight, we have a food addiction. The difference is that we cannot go through cold turkey (excuse the pun); we have to continue to eat and just like the alcoholic who takes the first drink, when we eat our first crisp, it is very hard not to keep on eating. There is even a taunting advert for crisps that challenges people – 'I bet you can't eat just one'.

How do we become addicted to food? Just like everything else – through our brain. We become addicted to food because our brain sends messages to our mouth about how good that piece of chocolate cake is going to taste. Think about something you love to eat right now. You will see a picture of it in your mind, whether it is a chocolate cake or a nice salad. The more you think about it, the more the picture stays in your mind, the more your mouth will begin to water, not for food, but for that specific food, for that specific taste. If you were simply hungry, the stomach would send messages to the brain; feed me, feed me, it's been a long time since you've sent any food down here! Most of the time we 'become' hungry for something because we've thought about it, or read about it or seen a picture of it on television; it is our brain that gives the message to our stomach, rather than the other way around.

This inner struggle to be the powerful one over food is, for most of us past the age of sixteen, a constant inner struggle, one which we fight all our lives. However, there are some who do gain control over food at an earlier age and then lose the control to the disease of anorexia.

Anorexia

Anorexia, in the beginning, is the opposite of being powerless. Anorexia is the ultimate in *control*. That is what is appealing to the anorexic; that is what draws her to this in the beginning and what sustains her far beyond the time when it is damaging to her body. An anorexic has control over food intake; she is more powerful than the food. Eventually, however, the anorexic loses control as the disease takes over and becomes the power; the anorexic becomes totally powerless against the strength of the disease; she is out of control.

There are non-psychological reasons for anorexia beginning, such as being on a gymnastic team or being a ballet dancer and therefore needing to keep one's weight very low. Apart from those types of reasons, it has been my experience that anorexics begin to control their food intake because it is the one thing that they can control in their life. If one's life is chaotic, if one is not made to feel power full at any time in one's life, then the fact that food intake can be carefully controlled is very satisfying.

Mary's problem began when she went away to college. For the first time in her life, no one was watching over what and how much she ate. Her parent's marriage was falling apart; they kept no secrets about their troubles from her, and she could not remember any time in her short life when she had been happy. Mary's life was out of control, from her perspective. Desperately wishing she could do something about her parents' marriage, desperately wanting to have a loving and united family, she went away to college feeling guilty for leaving. Maybe if she stayed, she could help, even though she never had been able to help before. Such were her irrational thoughts.

Mary was not very outgoing; she was quiet and shy. When the other girls on her floor in the dormitory were giggling and having a good time, being 'silly', Mary would try to join in, but couldn't. In many ways, she was more grown up than her peers and, because of that, she felt very isolated. At home, she at least had her mother to confide in, to feel close to, and although she did have a few casual friends, it was not the same; she would never have been able to tell them her inner feelings.

Without conscious awareness of it, Mary began over-eating; soon she had gained a few pounds. She was a tiny little thing anyway, but a few pounds kept her out of her favourite jeans and she grew alarmed. So she began to watch what she ate. Unlike Helen, she found this to be amazingly simple. She learned how many calories were in any food you could mention and she set a low goal for herself, a low number of calories per day. Sure enough, the extra weight came right off. Mary felt strangely proud of herself; she could control something, after all, and look how many people couldn't! She began to feel superior to the other young women who talked about losing weight while stuffing themselves at the same time.

After a while, Mary realised that it would be easier to make sure she never had more calories than she had decided on if she ate the same food every day, in the same quantity. Not only that, but she regulated when she ate each type of food. The problem was, she didn't eat very much and she grew thinner and thinner. At Christmas, her parents noticed how little she ate and how thin she was. By the spring holiday, they began to worry about her. When she came home for the summer, they dragged her, unwillingly, for help.

Mary, gradually, with set-backs here and there, got over her bout of anorexia, but the threat of it happening again, of her doing this to herself again, is ever present. The disease of anorexia still has the power. Six years later, she feels much more powerful than she did at the beginning of college. Six years and much therapy later, she has given up trying to help her parents' marriage and is relatively happy in her personal relationships. She is certainly not overweight, but she does eat healthily now and has come to the realisation that by taking good care of her body she is just as much in control as she distortingly thought she was when she so limited her food intake.

Bulimia

Bulimia also begins as a control issue. What a kick to be able to eat anything you want and not gain weight! When someone discovers how to do this (by throwing up right afterwards), she feels in control, much the way the anorexic does. A bulimic has learned a way she can have her cake and eat it too! But the bulimia is in control; not the bulimic. The disease of bulimia, just like alcohol or drugs, is in control of the addict. And soon, the compulsion to binge and purge becomes the powerful one and the bulimic is powerless.

Bulimics are harder to spot than anorexics. It is a secret disease; the bulimic is so ashamed of what she is doing, so afraid that others will find out, that she never tells anyone (other than a therapist when she finally comes for help). She not only never tells anyone, very often her spouse or lover or house mate knows nothing about it. Even in therapy, it has been my experience that the bulimic comes into therapy for some other situation and only after months of building up trust in the therapist, does she reveal this problem. (I am using the pronoun 'she' when speaking of these eating disorders because they are far more common in women than in men. Only one out of fifteen anorexics are male and bulimia also affects females more than males, although there are no exact figures for bulimia.)[9] Bulimics are able to keep their secret for years because, generally, they appear to be normal in weight. They, of course, do not think their weight is normal. Since they do not starve themselves and since most of them do not become hugely overweight, no one suspects.

Jeanette's problem began with the breakup of a relationship. Lonely and broken-hearted, she would go to the shop and buy any kind of pastry and cookies she could find. As the night came and darkness made her tiny flat seem even smaller, and yet, empty, she would park herself in front of the television, mindlessly watching any programme that might serve to divert her from her obsessive thinking about her lost boyfriend. She would sit there and eat. And eat. And eat. This is the binge part of the binge-and-purge cycle. A bulimic does not just overeat; she binges, usually on sweets. Jeanette got some satisfaction, temporarily, from this eating binge. 'I am going to treat myself; I've been treated so badly, I'm going to do something I want to do.' So goes the rebellious spirit inside, desperately trying to regain some power.

Next comes the guilt. 'What have I done? I'm going to weigh a ton!' Then the idea comes into her head that she can just get rid of it all before any damage is done. Usually, this idea comes into her head because she has read about someone doing this or has seen a programme about it on television, but sometimes it is an original idea.

At first, the bulimic may be rather proud of herself; she has found a way to enjoy her favourite foods and not gain weight. She feels she has conquered food; she is powerful! However, just as in the disease of anorexia, the disease of bulimia soon becomes the powerful one and the bulimic is powerless over the disease. Soon she seems to have no control over her binges and purges; they seem to have a life of their own; they are powerful and she is powerless. The addiction is in control.

Both of these eating disorders are very serious, anorexia is life-threatening and bulimia is extremely damaging to one's health. The psychological aspects are different in these two diseases. Anorexics are in extreme denial about the state of their body and how they look; they actually believe they look good when they are down to skeletal weight. This is why the disease is life-threatening; they do not want help; they want to continue losing weight. The bulimic, however, does eventually want help, for bulimics have a loathing for themselves that takes years to over-come, years after they have recovered. Both diseases are power draining. Anorexics need professional help to get well; they need medical as well as psychological help. But bulimics can and often do overcome their problem through self-help groups such as Bulimics Anonymous.

Alcohol, drugs

Alcohol and drugs are supreme controllers; they control a person's life, making the addict totally powerless. Many claim that alcohol makes them feel powerful, gives them courage. A drink or two probably does accomplish this, but an alcoholic cannot stop at one or two drinks and a drug addict must soon have another fix.

Alcohol is a legal drug and therefore almost everyone, at some time in their life, is exposed to it. However, some people can drink and others cannot. This doesn't seem fair, but research has shown a very close link between genetics and alcohol addition. Children of alcoholics are four times more vulnerable to alcohol addiction than are those who have no alcoholic parent. Having said that, it is my observation and belief that anyone can become an alcoholic, genetics or no. Alcohol creeps up on a person. The one pint of lager can slip over into one and a half and then on to two and so on. Our bodies develop a tolerance for alcohol, which means it takes more and more of it to have any effect. Even if there is no genetic predisposition, if someone drinks enough, often enough, alcoholism can be the result.

Why do we become addicted?

Why do we do these things to ourselves? I think it is very important in each kind of addiction and in each individual case to ferret out the reasons. When a young person tries a drug, there may not be any deep-rooted reason; he or she is probably doing it because 'everyone else is'. To teens or pre-teens and even on into university age, it is often more important to belong than anything else. To not be part of the group, to risk alienation, because of higher standards, takes a great deal of courage.

Low self-esteem is one of the major characteristics of drug users.[10] People who do not think much of themselves (i.e. are power empty) are often more vulnerable to peer pressure because they want desperately to be accepted and to belong. I do not believe anyone ever said to himself, 'I'm

going to begin taking drugs so that I can become addicted.'
It is much like death; we don't really think it will happen to
us.

Besides peer pressure, many young people seek thrills. It
is part of adolescence, part of becoming a person.
According to one expert, boredom is one reason why kids
say they use drugs. 'There's nothing better to do.' Some
psychologists believe that television may be at least partly
to blame. Children who grow up watching too much television have been found to have shorter attention spans and
to become bored more easily.[11]

Drug addicts speak of a 'rush' when they take a drug;
they like that feeling, it makes them feel powerful. The
problem is, those good feelings don't last. Far too soon, the
addiction is what controls them and life becomes one long
search to duplicate those good feelings they remember
from the beginning.

We now know there are physiological reasons for addictions. There are receptors in our brain called pleasure
receptors; these receptors are the mechanism by which
drugs such as cocaine and cigarettes become addicting.
The brain signals to the addict that he wants more; this is
the mechanism of craving. The addict becomes powerless
against the unbelievable pull on his life the drug has
created; not only in his physical body, but in his mind.[12]

Peter's story

Peter is one of the nicest chaps I know. He's the type one
would call the salt of the earth; he would do anything for
anybody. Active in my church, he attends the weekly prayer
meetings, where he has no patience for 'churchiness' and
talks to God as if he would to a mate of his, sitting there in
the prayer circle. But Peter was not always thought of so

highly, for Peter is a changed man – just ask his family. If
you went with Peter to his other weekly meeting, you
would hear him say in his Yorkshire accent, 'Hello, my
name is Peter and I am an alcoholic.' His other weekly
meeting is Alcoholics Anonymous.

Peter's story is long, as are most alcoholics' stories. His
job required that he entertain clients, so there were many
nights spent drinking in restaurants and pubs. He remembers the first time he discovered that taking a drink in the
morning helped, helped the hangover from the night
before. He tells of jobs lost, of car accidents, of broken
bones, of brushes with the police. Several times he was sent
for psychiatric help, sent by employers trying to help him.
But since he lied to the psychiatrists about his drinking –
'I told them I had two pints a day, instead of twelve!' – since
no one seemed to realise what the real problem was, Peter
went on and on, drinking more and more to get the 'high'
he so desperately sought. Through all these obvious problems, he was still in denial; he never blamed his job losses
or problems at home on drinking. There was a period
when he did not work for two years, but, 'There were four
million people out of work in Britain at the time – it was
not my fault I didn't have a job – it was the government,
the economy, lots of people didn't have jobs.' So Peter was
able to delude himself as well as others.

At one point during these years, Peter's wife Mary began
going to Al-Anon, the support group for family members
of AA. The meetings were on Saturday night and there was
an AA meeting right next door, held at the same time.
Tired of being left home alone on Saturday nights, Peter
began going to AA. He went there almost every Saturday
night for five years – while he was still drinking. How did
he get away with it, still drinking and attending meetings?

Peter was a 'bout' drinker, a binge drinker. He could and

often did go for long periods of time without drinking. One definition of an alcoholic is 'what happens when you take your first drink'. An alcoholic cannot stop. The first drink does it – they are off again on another bout of drinking. These bouts can be short or long, but eventually they end and the alcoholic is filled with remorse, promises his wife he will never drink again, and whether she believes him or not – he believes himself. So most of the time when Peter went to an AA meeting, he was sober. 'But I knew all about AA,' he told me. 'I could quote all the literature, I even gave people advice.' Peter talked the talk, but he did not walk the walk.

Alcoholism isn't funny, but one funny story Peter tells is about an outpatient therapy group he had been assigned to go to at a local mental health facility. 'I always came dressed up, in a shirt, tie and jacket', he says. 'One day I got there early, before the doctor arrived, and took the group out to the pub. They thought I was the doctor!'

Finally, after years of chaos, deteriorating health, and job and family problems, Mary began applying the Al-Anon programme in earnest. 'She moved the goal posts on me,' says Peter. Mary, like most family members of alcoholics, had always thought she could stop Peter's drinking. She would empty bottles down the sink when she found them, she would threaten to leave him, she tried to obstruct his self-destructive life. Al-Anon taught her to take care of herself instead. Al-Anon taught her to stop enabling Peter, to let him drink. And it worked – when she changed the rules of the game, the game that spouses of alcoholics play, the game of pleading and threatening and despairing, when the pattern of behaviour is changed, this often gets the alcoholic's attention. He would try to pick a fight and Mary would simply walk away. He would ask her to buy him a bottle of vodka and she would do it. He didn't know what to think. After one particularly bad bout, he promised he would go to an alcohol rehabilitation programme if he ever drank again. He didn't think he would ever need to go there, as always 'I thought I would never drink again'. But of course, he did.

Peter checked himself into an alcohol-treatment hospital in Weston-super-Mare. 'I thought I was going for a beach holiday,' he says. He soon found out this was no holiday, however. It was serious business, this getting sober, getting well, being restored to life. The programme at this hospital was staffed by recovering alcoholics, an essential need. Only recovering alcoholics can really understand what it feels like to be an alcoholic and, what is more important, a drinking alcoholic will only listen to someone who has been there, been through the same things, had the same feelings. Also, this programme was built on the first five steps of AA's Twelve Step Programme. The first five steps are as follows (loosely paraphrased).

1. Admit I am powerless over alcohol (or drugs, or food, or gambling) and my life has become unmanageable.
2. Believe a power greater than myself can restore me to sanity.
3. Make a decision to turn my will and my life over to the care of God as I understand him.
4. Make a searching and fearless moral inventory of myself.
5. Admit to God, to myself and to another human being, the nature of my wrongs.

Peter spent six weeks in that hospital. When he went back home, he began regularly attending AA meetings. He had a couple of relapses, very short bouts, but today he has nine years of sobriety and is very active in AA, helping others, 'giving back'.

He says he knows God was looking after him all those years; 'I should have been dead many times, with all my escapades'. Peter was brought up going to Sunday School; he knew 'the God of the Church' as he puts it, but when he and Mary were married, they didn't go to church – 'Too busy, you see'. At one point in his drinking a Methodist minister tried, in vain, to help him, and the family attended church. But it was through AA that Peter met God again. And now he is becoming reacquainted with the 'Church God' as he calls him.

Attending an AA meeting is a very spiritual experience. The basic tenet of AA is that there can be no recovery without turning one's life over to God; there has to be a spiritual experience, not just a spiritual belief. *The Big Book*, the basic book put out by Alcoholics Anonymous, tells inspirational story after story about those who have achieved sobriety. In other words, the organisation clearly states that not only is the addict powerless over the alcohol, he or she is powerless without God. They do not preach Christianity as such, they speak of turning to one's higher power as one understands him. Stating it this way keeps a barrier from forming if a person has some prejudices against the Church. What often happens is that in the process of recovering, in turning himself over to God, God reveals himself to the addict. He or she feels God's love and guiding, and in my experience, goes on to become acquainted with the fullness of God in the Trinity.

The power of the group is one reason why Alcoholics Anonymous works. Those who attend AA meetings are accepted, made to feel they belong; there is power in the group support that is very important to their recovery. However, if all that were needed to recover were other people who were in the same circumstances, there would be no need for a higher power. Power is an important word in recovery from addictions. Admitting one is powerless over the addiction and at the same time, turning one's life over to a higher power are keystones of the AA movement.

Recovering

I thoroughly enjoy knowing recovering alcoholics. They are honest, open and caring people. They have done serious work on themselves and let God work on them much more than the general population. Recovering and because of recovering, coming to know God, has been the means for many to become power full.

A recovering alcoholic is supposed to be always working on himself. I maintain that all of us, whatever our problem, are recovering human beings and should continually work on ourselves, in order to love and be loved, in order to become and remain power full.

CHAPTER 8

DEPRESSION AND ANXIETY

Depression and anxiety are two more forms of inner struggles. Those suffering from these two emotional illnesses feel powerless to do anything about it. Some situational depressions eventually go their course and the afflicted person begins to feel better, but serious depression and anxiety disorders nearly always need professional help.

Depression

The three words psychologists use to describe how a person who is suffering from depression feels are _hopeless_, _helpless_ and _worthless._ I would add to this the word _powerless._

A depressed person may not think of himself as _depressed_; he applies these adjectives to himself instead. Those words are a description of how he feels. He feels worth less than he used to be, which indicates past behaviour. He feels helpless, unable to help himself now, in the present. And he feels hopeless, he has no hope for the future. This takes care of all time frames; past, present and future. No wonder he feels boxed in, power empty, insecure within himself and with others.

A depressed person has been power drained. This may be due to some kind of loss, whether it be the loss of a love, a job, reputation or even something material. If a person is power full and loses a loved one, either through death or divorce or rejection, then that person will, of course, be sad, upset and may become depressed. However, unless the depression is clinical, which needs medication to be remedied, that person will, after a time, return to their former emotionally balanced state. Not because they did not love that person and not because they were hard hearted, but simply because although there is an empty space in their lives; in themselves, they are not empty.

There is a big difference between feeling empty and being empty. Everyone, even those who are the most power full, gets an empty feeling now and then, feels sad or lonely. The difference is that power-full people spring back from adversity much more quickly and are able to get on with their life.

There are two kinds of depression. There is situational depression, where one has suffered a loss and feels 'down'. If after a few months these feelings have not begun to improve, professional or pastoral counselling would be helpful. Then there is the far more serious kind of depression, clinical depression, called endogenous (*en* meaning in; in the body) which renders the person much more powerless than the situational depression I just spoke of. Clinical depression can occur even if someone is power full. It is often an inherited predisposition; there may be a family history of depression. In these cases, medication is essential. Therapy is very useful to teach the patient how to deal with his distorted thoughts, but clinical depression is too serious to be dealt with by therapy alone. The reason for this is physical, not psychological.

When a person is clinically depressed, has symptoms

such as sleep problems, appetite problems, and/or a lack of concentration, it is a sign that the mood-altering chemicals in the brain are not producing as they should. Our moods are affected by certain chemicals in the brain and when there is a depletion of those chemicals, the result can be depression. Anti-depressant medications give the system a 'jump-start', get those chemicals going again. Many people are reluctant to begin taking anti-depressants; they do not like the idea of taking drugs and are afraid of becoming addicted. But anti-depressants are not addictive, as are tranquillisers. I like to use the analogy of insulin. If a person is a diabetic, his body has a shortage of insulin and therefore it is essential to that person's health to take that drug. It is the same with clinical depression. It may be essential for that person; there may be a shortage of the necessary chemicals in the brain to lift that person out of depression. Situational depression, however, either eventually goes away or is managed adequately by short-term counselling.

John, whose story was told in the chapter on relationships, became more and more depressed as his former success slipped away. He became lethargic; he began to watch television during the day when he would ordinarily have been out making calls on clients. Before his sales started declining, John had been fairly athletic. He and Julia had met at a gym where they both worked out three times a week. He used to play basketball with a group of friends from college. Now, when they called him to play, he would make some excuse. It wasn't so much that he did not want to play; he just did not want to face his friends who were all doing so well in their jobs, or at least he assumed they were, since no one said anything to the contrary. He felt like a failure and it was easier for him to avoid seeing old friends. If someone had asked how he was doing with his sales, he probably would have been evasive and given them the impression that everything was fine.

John had entered the downward spiral of depression. An event occurs, in this case the decline in sales of new insurance policies. He began to lose confidence in his ability to sell. As he began to lose his confidence, he actually was not selling as well, which simply reinforced his thinking about his ability. As he became more dejected, he wasn't as pleasant to be around as he had been before. This affected his relationship with Julia, so he began to think that she did not love him any more. Down and down he went.

How does this actually happen? What is the mechanism that triggers this lack of confidence? It is our thinking process. Our feelings are caused by our thoughts. If I say to myself, 'Why am I writing this book? No one is going to read it; I am wasting my time!' then I may very well stop writing. I have the power within to make myself lose confidence, even with no outside input.

John, however, did have outside input. His sales had plummeted. There was concrete evidence that he was not as good at selling as he had been previously. But was that correct? 'I am not selling as well as I did previously' is an interpretation of the event; other interpretations are possible. There was a recession on – cars, homes and furniture were also not selling as well as before. John, however, took onto himself the entire blame and as he kept on giving himself these negative messages, his feelings plummeted just as his sales did. You will remember that his wife, Julia, was very successful in her job. This added to his negativity. Rather than being glad that at least one of them was making a good living, Julia's success made John feel even more like a failure. Julia insisted that John get help. This is fairly typical; a depressed person often doesn't have the energy, the initiative, to help himself or herself. Much of the time it is a family member who initiates treatment.

The first thing John needed to do was just talk. And talk. That was the genius of Freud; he was the first to discover that people felt better if they were simply allowed to vent, to talk without interruption, to say anything they pleased, to 'get everything off their chest'. Very soon in the therapy, however, I began to teach John the principles of Cognitive Therapy.

This method is based on the theory that all our feelings are caused by our thoughts, that everything depends upon perception. There are many methods of doing therapy, many theories, but since this book is about becoming power full, not about therapy, and since the kind of therapy I do is called Cognitive, this is the way I will describe how therapy can help someone who is depressed and therefore feels far down on the continuum of power.

It's all in your mind!

It's all in your mind! Has anyone ever said that to you? Have you ever accused anyone else of that? It's all in your mind, meaning, in the popular usage of that phrase, what you believe, or think, or are worried about, isn't really so. You are making it up, is the connotation; the reality is one thing and what you are thinking is another. It's all in your mind.

Well, they, or you, were right. It is all in your mind. Not only the reality, but also what we are thinking, what we are feeling, are also 'all in our mind'. Why? Because that is the only place where any of our interpretations of reality, our perceptions, can be. That does not necessarily mean, though, that what we are thinking isn't true. What is in your mind may be the absolute correct view of the facts, yet if those facts are painful, it can lead to a lessening of power and in cases where what we are thinking is not the reality, it can lead to a lessening of power needlessly.

It all depends on your point of view. If my husband planned to play golf and it began to rain, he might be upset by this weather, but if I had just planted flower seeds in my garden, I will be thrilled to see a good shower. Our expectations, our view of the event called rain would be very different. Using the analogy of the house we were building, if I like antiques and old houses, I will look at a modern house with different eyes than someone who very much likes the modern look and would feel very uncomfortable in an old-fashioned house. When we see something, each of us puts it into the framework of our own peculiar outlook, peculiar not because it is strange, but because it is ours alone.

The Bible has a lot to say about how we should think. In Ephesians 4:23, Paul tells us to 'be made new in the attitude of your minds' and again, in Romans 12:2, he instructs us to 'be transformed by the renewing of your mind'. How do we actually go about this? How do we change our attitudes; how do we renew our mind?

By changing our thoughts. I began teaching John to notice his negative thoughts. That means to recognise and write down all the negative things one is saying to oneself all day long. Depressed people think in distorted ways, they see the world and themselves in such negative dimensions that their very thinking processes bring their mood down. This is called distorted thinking. Cognitive therapy does not teach people to think positively; instead it teaches people to think realistically, to challenge their negative thinking, thought by thought. The following is an example of what John might have been thinking about himself when he was depressed.

Stages of Cognitive Therapy

'I'm no good as a salesman. My previous sales records were a fluke. I'll never be able to sell again.'

In the book, *Feeling Good*, David Burns lists ten cognitive distortions. These three examples of John's negative thinking fit into three of those distortions. 'I'm no good as a salesman' is an example of Labelling; John was giving himself the label of a poor salesman. The realistic thought would be 'I haven't been selling as well lately'. We often label ourselves and others, depressed or not, but a depressed person usually has many negative labels for himself. The next statement, 'My previous sales records were a fluke' is called Disqualifying the Positive, distorting the truth about ourselves. John took a proven fact, his past sales records, and disqualified it, told himself it meant nothing. And 'I'll never be able to sell again' is a Fortune Telling Statement – John is predicting the future. None of us can predict the future. By telling himself he would never be able to sell again, John is contributing greatly to his depression; he is frightening himself and when taken to the extreme, this type of thinking becomes a self-fulfilling prophecy.[13]

As you read this, you probably recognise that you sometimes make these same kinds of distorted judgements about yourself. Depressed or not, we all do this. The difference is that if a person is depressed, this type of thinking is pervasive; it goes on all day and night, and when something good does happen, it is not interpreted as being good. A severely depressed person cannot experience joy or laughter or any of the power-filling things that might make him feel better.

Our automatic negative thoughts are simply the first layer of our thinking process. Underneath those are what are called Basic Assumptions. Again, we all have these; some are negative and some are positive. Basic assumptions can begin with the word 'if'. 'If I keep on not making any money, Julia is going to leave me' was one of John's thoughts. 'If I can no longer sell, there isn't any other career for me' was another. 'If I was making lots of money, Julia would respect me.' The list went on and on. It can be seen from these few examples that our basic assumptions about ourselves and others have a more serious effect on us than the top layer, the more obvious negative thoughts. These take longer to get to than the first, because they are deeper, more an embedded part of our personality.

Then there is yet another layer to our thinking process – our core beliefs. Core beliefs are what we think of ourselves. They usually begin with 'I'. 'I'm a failure, I'm thick, I'm no good . . . .' These core beliefs take even longer to uncover. It is here, at this level of core beliefs, that the therapy becomes meaningful.

Negative thinking does not cause depression, but negative thinking is a symptom of depression; these negative thoughts render a person more and more powerless. Teaching someone to challenge those negative thoughts, one by one, is a vital step in pulling oneself out of depression.

John's depression was treated successfully by therapy alone; he did not need medication. However, if his depression had continued and if he had begun to have suicidal thoughts, I would have immediately referred him to a psychiatrist for anti-depressant medication and perhaps would have hospitalised him until the danger was past.

Depression is a supreme power drainer and very dangerous. Only a professional can correctly diagnose depression and anyone who has someone in their family who they think may be depressed, must, at all costs, seek help for him or her. Cognitive therapy can teach the person how to pull out of the depression and how to recognise a recurrence. If medication is necessary, cognitive therapy is still very useful, especially after the medication has begun to work, clearing the person's mind of the confusion caused by the depression to enable them to understand what they are doing to themself and how to help themself.

Anxiety

If depression makes us lethargic and sluggish, it would seem that anxiety would be just the opposite – stirred up and restless. In some ways that is true, but anxiety is not the exact opposite of depression; in many ways the two conditions are similar.

When someone is experiencing a panic attack, he feels totally powerless, just as a depressed person does. He feels powerless over the anxiety. The anxiety has taken over, is in control, and he feels that he has no power to do anything about it whatsoever.

Irv was forty-five when he had his first panic attack. He was in a lift, going up to the fourth floor to his office, the same lift he took day after day. Suddenly, his heart began racing; he broke out in a cold sweat; he felt as if he was going to black out. He panicked. Who wouldn't at a time like that? 'I was sure I was going to die, right there in the lift,' he told me, months later when he had finally come for psychological help with what he was still certain was a medical problem.

'I was sure I was having a heart attack. The lift stopped and I gasped for help from the couple who were about to get on the lift.' They kindly escorted Irv to the nearest office, where he sat down while an ambulance was called. But by the time the ambulance arrived, Irv felt perfectly all right. He went to casualty anyway, certain that what he had suffered was the beginning of a heart problem. All the tests were negative; he was told that the feelings were probably due to stress and he should relax more.

Irv was not convinced. And the next day, when he got in the same lift and the same sequence of events occurred, he really wasn't convinced. This time, he got off the lift on his floor and slowly made it to his office, where he soon began to feel all right. Irv stopped taking the lift; he began to avoid any lifts, climbing the stairs instead. This is how agoraphobia begins. A person will start avoiding all situations where panic attacks occur, until it finally gets to the point where one feels too frightened to leave home.

Irv set himself up for a thorough cardiovascular work-up that same week. The results were the same – negative. His doctor explained to him the physiological nature of panic attacks and told him he wanted him to see a psychiatrist for medication which might prevent further attacks. The problem with the medication is that it is addictive, unlike anti-depressants, which are not. The medicine will mask the problems and in severe cases is often necessary temporarily, but therapy or education is essential to teach the sufferer how to deal with the anxiety and panic attacks.

Irv needed to learn how to 'talk himself down' when he had these attacks, how to distract himself and wait them out. Learning these techniques, through Cognitive Therapy, gave him his power back. As long as he let the panic take over, he was powerless. When he learned that he really could control the anxiety, could make the symptoms diminish, could even prevent them from occurring, he regained his power. Education about the nature of panic attacks is the first step and the most important one.

Panic-attack victims are always amazed when a therapist or another panic-attack victim describes their symptoms so perfectly. 'How did you know?' they always ask. We know because the symptoms are always similar. That is why education is so important; vital in this problem. The first thing I do for a person who is experiencing panic attacks is give him or her a book about panic attacks. I tell him or her to read it and then to read it again and then to read it again. In the pages of a book about panic attacks, the victim will read all about his or her symptoms and how to overcome them.

I advised Irv to count when he felt a panic attack coming on. There was a large green plant in a pot in my office. 'Count the leaves on that plant,' I told him. When he finished, I would ask, 'Are you sure? Count them again.' The first time I did this, he told me afterwards that he thought I was the one who was crazy! What I was having Irv do is called Distraction. No matter where you are, there is something you can count. The tiles on the floor, the stripes on the wallpaper, the letters in an advert on the tube. Becoming obsessed with counting anything is a tool to fool the mind and body. As awareness of the frightening symptoms going on in one's body diminishes, as one stops paying attention to them, the symptoms will go away sooner. Counting is one way to do this. Another way is to learn to relax and breathe properly. Taking a long, slow, deep breath and then exhaling the breath slowly is a relaxation method that will help at the time of the panic attack.

There is much more detail that a panic-attack victim needs to learn; self-help groups for this problem are very beneficial, as well as therapy. Panic attacks are not due to some deep, psychological hurt one experienced in childhood. As in depression, some people are anxiety prone and others are not. Stress can and often does bring on the feelings; it is not so important in this case to find out why; it is more important to do something about them.

Anxiety and depression are complicated subjects that I have skimmed over here, but they are definitely inner struggles, inner struggles for power over one's mind and body. Just like addictions, these problems can and usually do become powerful and can render the struggler powerless. Getting qualified help, resolving the problem, will release the sufferer to get on with life, freed from either of these frightening afflictions.

Clients are always relieved when I tell them that depression and/or anxiety are not mental illnesses, rather they are emotional illnesses. Emotional illnesses, while quite serious, are far less serious than mental illnesses.

Paul tells us in Phillipians 4:8–9:

> Finally, brothers, whatever is true, whatever is noble, whatever is right, whatever is pure, whatever is lovely, whatever is admirable – if anything is excellent or praiseworthy – think about such things. Whatever you have learned or received or heard from me, or seen in me – put it into practice. And the God of peace will be with you.

Think about such things. It is hard to think about such things when depression or anxiety is flooding one's brain with feelings of powerlessness. It is hard to think about such things when one is power empty. It is difficult to experience the God of peace at such times, even though he is there. Emotions have flooded the brain and it is hard to think about lovely things.

Notice that Paul did not say 'feel' about these things; he told us to think. Changing our thinking will change our feelings. Changing our thinking will allow our head to rule over these destructive emotions, freeing us to feel the good, freeing us to experience the God of Peace.

CHAPTER 9

ANGER AND POWER

Charlene was referred to me by her doctor. She had gone to see her, asking for tranquillisers to 'calm her down'. Rather than just prescribe, Charlene's doctor had wisely required a psychological evaluation before starting her on an addictive drug.

Charlene's problem was an explosive temper that got her into trouble with her employees as well as in relationships. Successful, bright and energetic, Charlene began her career as a secretary and now ten years later owned a secretarial agency. She worked hard and expected her employees to work hard too. She loved being the boss, being the one who runs things rather than being the one who is told what to do, but whenever she was crossed, or questioned, or even if one of her employees showed a little bit of independence in thinking, Charlene would explode. She became known as 'Charlene the terrible', and because of her temper, she had a large turnover in personnel.

'I think my problem is stress,' she told me. 'I don't know how to relax. I haven't gone on holiday for ten years. My business is my whole life and I guess it's just getting to be too much for me.' She looked at me earnestly, 'I don't think

I need to see a psychologist; I think I just need to go to Florida!' Charlene went on to say that if she could get more sleep at night and learn to relax (with the help of the pills) these incidents would not occur and her business would be less stressful.

However, the business was not the only problem. Charlene had also never been able to sustain a long-term relationship. Within two or three weeks of going out with someone, she would get angry about something he said and either let him know it or just keep it inside. Either way, the result was the same. Whether the man lost interest in her, or she lost interest in him, relationships never developed.

Until now, this problem had not bothered Charlene too much. She had been so busy building her business and was so tired when she wasn't working that whether she had a relationship or not didn't matter much. Now, at the age of thirty-five, the biological clock was ticking and since she had reached her goals, she really did want something more than work.

It was true that Charlene was suffering from stress and it was obvious that she had a problem with anger. I taught her relaxation exercises and urged her to meditate once a day to relieve her stress. This helped, at least for a little while after she had done the exercises. Her body and mind slowed down and benefited by this respite for an hour a day. However, I did not believe her anger was caused by stress. When I asked her why she hadn't gone on holiday for ten years, she said, 'I would be bored to death! Lying on a beach somewhere is not for me and I hate museums – I don't know, it just sounds so . . .' (Charlene hesitated, looking for the right word) 'purposeless!' she finally burst out. Charlene was a power-driven person, but that was not her problem. She loved what she did; she loved the challenge of her business. Charlene's problem was anger.

Causes of anger

If life is a struggle for power, then anger is the supreme manifestation of that struggle. Power, or lack of it, and anger are integrally entwined. When someone gets angry, negative power begins to fill that person's mind; when he or she expreses the anger, a negative energy permeates the air, just like pollution. When we get angry, we either act out that anger (by yelling at someone or telling someone off or actually hurting them physically), or we keep the anger inside and struggle within ourselves with feelings of powerlessness. Anger can be either an inner struggle or an outer struggle with someone else and often it is both. When we are alone, we have an inner struggle about our powerlessness over anger and when we are with the person who makes us angry, it is an interactional power struggle. Most of the time, most of us will not display the anger to someone who, for whatever reason, is higher on the continuum of power in relation to us. We act differently with different people depending upon how we relate to them in terms of power.

A power-full person is not often struggling for power, therefore is able to interpret events as they really are, unemotionally and rationally, and is able to deal with each one without getting angry. Only a person who is power full is able to keep from engaging in a power struggle, particularly if he or she is in a higher position on the continuum of power than the person he or she is dealing with. To have power and not use it shows a well-adjusted person, peaceful within oneself.

It appears to me that powerlessness creates more anger

than does power. In fact, having power does not 'create' anger at all. Rather, the anger is created by something that happens, by what someone is thinking, remembering or interpreting about the event. Having power does, however, determine whether the anger will be shown. If I am bigger and stronger than you and if I am prone to showing my anger physically, I will be much more likely to hurt you physically than if you are bigger and stronger than I am. If you are my boss and you are angry at me, you will be more likely to let me know you are angry than if I am the boss and you are the employee. The more power, the more likelihood it will be shown, acted out, to those with less power. However, the power itself does not create the anger.

Powerlessness, on the other hand, does create anger. Whether it is a sense of being unfairly blamed, or a feeling of a lack of control, or the inability to do anything about a situation, powerlessness often engenders rage.

All of us experience both situations. There are some whom we have power over and others who have power over us, but everyone does not get angry easily (or at all) just because he or she might have power over someone. And there are those who never appear to get angry; there are people who say, 'I don't get angry; I only get hurt.'

Sources

How do we get where we are in terms of our anger threshold? Why do some people experience hair-trigger anger while others have infinite patience and must really be deliberately provoked before losing their temper?

Anger is born in childhood. Just like all other personality characteristics, how we handle anger, how we display it, or how we feel about it, comes from two sources – learning and genetic predispositions, the framework and the foundation. There are children, even infants, who right from the start appear to be easily angered, who have temper tantrums, who are quickly frustrated. These infants appear to be born with an angry personality. Many parents feel out of control, powerless, in the face of these children's anger; they don't know how to handle it. Having said that, it is still my belief that most anger is learned. Even when the genetic predisposition is there, the tendency towards anger can be softened, depending upon the learning, or conversely, it can be promoted, albeit usually unwittingly.

If Mum slams the kitchen cupboard doors when she is mad at Dad, her daughter will probably grow up and slam kitchen cupboard doors, even if as a child she vowed to herself that she would never get angry with her husband and she certainly wouldn't get angry in front of her child and even then, she for sure wouldn't slam doors! Yet five years into her marriage, she one day finds herself slamming cupboard doors in front of her wide-eyed little girl and is dismayed.

We seem doomed to repeat what we learned as a child. Using Jim from the fourth chapter as an example, when he was married he watched with amazement the first time his young wife, whom he loved dearly, blow up at him over some trivial matter. It was not that he hadn't experienced anger, but he had not experienced it in his home; it was not part of his repertoire.

His wife had not grown up in such idyllic circumstances. Her parents had fought often and loudly. It was true she hated it as a child and just like the mother mentioned above, had vowed she would never do it, but it was part of her repertoire, the framework of her personality. It was something she had observed, experienced, learned, and, when she became irritated, she displayed her anger in the same way she had observed it.

Child abuse

Worse yet, in terms of consequences, if someone was physically or emotionally abused as a child, statistics show that he or she has a much, much greater chance of abusing his or her own children than if this had not happened. Why? Because she experienced it; it is part of her repertoire; the actions, words, were stamped into her brain. All children, in reality, are at the mercy of their parents, at the mercy of the adult world, and therefore, at least positionally, are powerless. So that if a child suffers abuse, that child as an adult has a good chance of abusing his own children as a way to gain power. Not because he or she thinks it is right, but because it is part of that person's repertoire, part of what he or she learned when growing up.

Child abuse is caused by a feeling of powerlessness, even though it may appear to be the opposite – the abuse of power by the parent, who is larger and stronger. Parents and/or caretakers do have tremendous power over children. For most, this realisation is scary. The responsibility of being so influential, of directing a child's life, is tremendous. For some, becoming a parent is the very first time they have ever had any power; it is a chance to have complete control. When that control is threatened, when lack of control is interpreted as a power struggle, child abuse can occur.

Carla was referred to a family crisis centre where I was an intern many years ago. She was seventeen, slim and pretty as any teenager one would expect to see in the classrooms of a high school. But Carla was not in school; she had a three-month-old baby boy and she was living on welfare. It was her social worker at the welfare office who had referred her to us for help.

'I just can't do it!' Carla told me. 'I just can't handle the baby's crying!' she went on. Carla had not hurt her baby yet; she had not physically abused him for doing what comes very naturally to babies, crying, but she probably would have if she had not come for help. Carla felt very isolated, lonely and inept. Carla's mother tried to help, but she was working all day and needed her sleep at night. Her boyfriend, the baby's father, just wanted peace and quiet when he came home in the evening from working on a construction project. Besides, he was as clueless as Carla about how to take care of a baby. Carla felt overwhelmed.

Child abuse happens because of feelings of powerlessness, what may feel like a power struggle between the child and the parent. Maybe it happens the first time the baby cries uncontrollably, will not stop crying. The helplessness the adult feels when he cannot do anything to make the child stop crying, is a powerless feeling and can lead to rage, a rage that can manifest itself as physical or emotional child abuse. In actuality, there is no power struggle between an infant and an adult, at least on the part of the infant. An infant is not struggling for power; the infant is simply letting the world know that there is something he or she needs.

Carla, like many young parents, simply needed some emotional support and some lessons in parenting. She loved the baby and did not want to hurt him, but her sense of powerlessness overwhelmed her at times. Through meeting once a week with other mothers in the same situation, by attending parenting classes at the agency, and by using the Child Abuse Hotline where volunteers talk to a parent who is about to lose control, she found the power she needed to bring up the baby without anger.

Power struggles

When Johnny doesn't clean up his room, or do his home-work, or fights with his sister, and his father blows up at him, what the father is doing, what motivates the dad, is the power struggle. Power struggles make us angry. From a parent's point of view, when a child doesn't obey, he is asserting himself over the parent's power. A parent's basic assumption about the parent-child relationship is that the parent is in charge; the parent makes the rules and the child obeys those rules. When this doesn't happen, the anger is caused by the parent's interpretation, 'I am losing or have already lost control here.' The 'should' in 'I should be in control of this child' causes the anger.

Power-empty persons will more often become angry when they feel their power threatened than those higher on the continuum of power. If their children are the only ones lower on the continuum in their lives, anger may be used as an unconscious means of staying in power.

Most crimes of passion are cases where one person feels powerless against another. Homicide is a desperate strug-gle to attain power and there is an auxiliary emotion involved, hatred. Hatred is a very strong, negative power; it envelops a person the same as love does and can. The expression 'consumed with hate' is very descriptive. The hateful and hate-filled thoughts consume, fill his or her mind, overpower him or her. Overpower, an interesting word. The hate is over the person's power, over, covering, in control and he or she, hence, tries to overpower the victim.

Psychotic killers are usually loners, people who have felt powerless in society in general, but in their own life in par-ticular, all their lives. In their solitude, they sit and think. And think. And think. Their anger grows and grows until it can erupt in a murder. In that small moment, they experience power over the victim; in the moment of destroying or hurting someone else, the psychotic has power, after feeling totally powerless most of his or her life. Power itself can become the goal and if the psychotic only knows one way to attain it, he may repeat. This is why it does not matter who the victim is; the victim is merely symbolic, a means to the end that is a rush of power. This kind of negative power will ultimately result in the psychotic's losing any chance for power, since ultimately he will be locked up – a truly powerless situation.

Rage

People do not have to be psychotic to go into a rage. Divorce is one situation that often causes very ordinary people to do some fairly desperate things. 'A man angry with his wife for filing for divorce obtained a demolition permit and bulldozed their new three-bedroomed home into oblivion while she was out of town. "I guess he didn't want me to have anything," said the wife.'" This story, in the *Los Angeles Times*, is an extreme example of rage. This soon to be ex-husband was so angry that short of physically harming his wife, he displayed his anger in a negatively powerful way.

Powerlessness is the main source of anger in divorces when one person leaves another, when the divorce was not mutual, as in the case described above. Anger can escalate to rage very easily and very quickly because the one who is left feels so out of control, so powerless to bring the other person back. Getting angry, however, does not put him in control.

When we are angry, we are out of control. Out of control means loss of power. We may gain negative power over someone we are angry at; he or she may be fearful of us because of that negative power, but we lose our own power in the act of expressing the anger. Even if we don't express the anger, we lose our inner power, disturb the peace, if you will, by remaining angry. Anger is a power drainer; the negative power that seems to fill us for a time can make us feel drained later, emotionally exhausted.

A small example of this is when we 'glare' at someone who has said something or done something that irritates us. Recently, my husband and I were in a street market and the owner of a fruit and vegetable stand was extremely rude to us. We just walked away, but I turned around and glared at the man! Very Christian of me . . . . That glare did not make me feel better and it actually robbed me of any power to deal with this man ever again. He was in the wrong, but I should have dealt with it in a more constructive manner; instead, I chose to summon up negative energy, which then affected me negatively. All negative emotions are power drainers in the end.

Resentment

If exploding in anger is an obvious power drainer, then resentment is the secret, hidden power drainer that to some degree bothers us all. The only difference between resentment and anger is that resentment is older; it is past tense; it is the chewing and mulling over of that deed, that remark, that festers and remains as resentment. Most of us are harbouring some kind of resentment most of the time, from little petty slights to having been victimised by someone in our earlier life. It hides itself deep within and like a worm, burrows its way into our personality.

We are often not aware of our resentment. Very seldom do you hear someone name it; very seldom do you hear someone say, 'I'm resentful!' Resentment is the result of one of two things: either a person has felt hurt rather than angry, and pushes the hurt down, which later becomes resentment, or a person feels angry and doesn't express it, pushing the anger down. The end result is resentment.

Early in my career as a psychologist, I became aware of how many people (predominately women) there were who said they do not get angry, that they just experience the pain of being hurt. I would have them list events as they happened each week, events which hurt them emotionally as well as events which made them angry. The purpose of this exercise was to get them to recognise that they actually did experience anger, but they labelled this feeling as hurt. When the 'hurt' was correctly labelled as anger, it was easier to work with in terms of change. Hurt implies being a victim, which translates as being powerless, but anger is less power draining and once identified can be dealt with on its own terms. This exercise was always very useful to those, as I said, mainly women, who had been interpreting events as hurt all their lives.

I found that most men were quick to find many experiences which they labelled as anger, yet had trouble recognising when they felt hurt. I do not believe this gender difference is due wholly to societal or learning factors. In this case, I think this is a gender difference built on differences in hormones. As I said in the chapter on male/female differences, little boys are naturally more aggressive than little girls, therefore anger is a more natural emotion.

Roots of Charlene's anger

We are often not aware of the real cause of our anger. If asked, most of us would say we got angry because of something someone said or did, but this is only partially true. Underlying that reason is a deeper one, one that needs to be rooted out, just as did Charlene's unreasonable anger with her employees.

Charlene grew up in a home where achieving was rewarded – rewarded by praise, rewarded by presents, and by a feeling of pride. And achieve she did. She was in the swimming team at high school and at college, having aspirations to be in the Olympics. Try as she might, Charlene never made it, so after three Olympic trials, she gave up. However, this drive with which she had been infused continued into her work as an adult.

This sounds good, does it not? Sounds as though she had support and approval from her parents. It is true she did not make the Olympics, but was that what she was resentful about? No, she had come to terms with her disappointment over that.

Charlene's resentment was caused by her parents' attitude towards her brother. While Charlene was at swimming practice every afternoon and studying to get good marks, Jason was getting out of one jam and into another, mostly because of his drug habit. It had begun with marijuana and grew into a fully fledged cocaine addiction. Charlene's parents were overwhelmed by his problems; as they grew worse, that seemed to be all they talked about. When Charlene was away at college, phone calls were filled with tales of Jason's latest escapades and began to be less centred around what Charlene was doing. From her point of view, the good things she was accomplishing were taken for granted; her parent's focus was all on Jason.

The seeds of resentment began to grow. Resentment came into full bloom when Mark entered a rehabilitation programme and successfully got clean and sober. Every time he did anything that was the least bit in the right direction, his parents raved and praised Jason, not only to him, but also to Charlene. When he got a job at a petrol station and did not leave or get fired, it was worthy of a news headline, or so Charlene felt. When he made some new friends who were not into drugs, there were more rave revues. It was the prodigal son story all over again and Charlene felt that her efforts all along meant nothing to her parents.

Charlene was not power full. She had been shown love and reward by her parents for doing, not for being. So when her 'doing' was seen as useless in terms of the praise being given Mark for what seemed to Charlene as very ordinary things, she was hurt, then resentful, and finally bitter. Yet she kept on achieving, because by now it was a habit, thoroughly ingrained. She kept on trying to win love and approval by doing things, achieving, the only way she knew how.

Awareness of why she was on such a treadmill to achieve was very helpful to Charlene in understanding her anger, but she did not become a nice boss lady overnight. Anger becomes a habit and has to be dealt with behaviourally as well as cognitively. Once rooted out, the whys known, the habit still has to be dealt with.

Are we supposed to get angry?

What does Scripture say about anger? Are we supposed to get angry? Are we not supposed to turn the other cheek? If I still get angry, am I being a 'proper' Christian?

There are many verses in Proverbs that exhort us to be patient, to not be quickly provoked, to give a gentle answer when someone is angry with us, 'only fools give full vent to their anger'. James tells us: 'Everyone should be quick to listen, slow to speak and slow to become angry, for man's anger does not bring about the righteous life that God desires' (James 1:19–20). And Paul tells us to get rid of 'anger, rage, malice, slander' (Colossians 3:8).

Jesus said:

> You have heard that it was said to the people long ago, 'Do not murder, and anyone who murders will be subject to judgment. But I tell you that anyone who is angry with his brother will be subject to judgment. Again, anyone who says to his brother, 'Raca', is answerable to the Sanhedrin. But anyone who says, 'You fool!' will be in danger of the fire of hell.
>
> (Matthew 5:21–22)

We must not 'murder' someone with words, with anger. Jesus sounds very forceful in this; it does not sound like a suggestion to me. William Barclay, the Scottish theologian, wrote in-depth commentaries on the New Testament. He says:

> Long lasting anger is bad; contemptuous speaking is worse, and the careless or the malicious talk which destroys a man's good name is worst of all. So, then, Jesus insists that the gravest thing of all is to destroy a man's reputation and to take his good name away. No punishment is too severe for the malicious tale-bearer, or the gossip over the tea cups which murders people's reputations. The man who is the slave of anger, the man who speaks in the accent of contempt, the man who destroys another's good name, may never have committed a murder in action, but he is a murderer at heart.[14]

Barclay also says:

> There must be anger in the Christian life, but it must be the right kind of anger. There would be something essential missing in a man who had lost the faculty of being angry. Selfish anger, anger at what happens to oneself, is always wrong. Crossness and bad

temper and irritability are without defence. But there is an anger without which the world would be a poorer place.... There were times when Jesus was terribly and majestically angry. He was angry when the scribes and Pharisees were watching to see if He would heal the man with the withered hand on the Sabbath day. It was not their criticism of himself at which he was angry; he was angry that their rigid orthodoxy desired to impose unnecessary suffering on a fellow creature. He was angry when he made a whip and drove the changers of money and the sellers of victims from the Temple courts.... The anger which is selfish, passionate, undisciplined, uncontrolled is a sinful, a useless and a hurtful thing, which must be banished from the Christian life. But the anger which is disciplined into the service of Christ and our fellow men, and which is utterly pure and utterly selfless, is one of the great dynamic forces in this world.[15]

How we give up anger

How do we do this? How do we stop what may be a life-long habit, how do we 'give up' our anger? First, by identifying why we are angry. Very often, we are angry inappropriately. Very often we get angry because of a misunderstanding. We think someone meant one thing and he or she actually did not mean that at all. When we learn to talk about our anger or annoyance or resentment with the person we are angry with, we will often come away with an understanding of how each one of us, in our individualistic ways, becomes angry.

I have found working with clients that there are usually themes to our anger, particularly with married couples. Anger is usually based on our basic assumptions about ourselves and others. If a wife assumes that her husband does not think he should do housework, then every time he doesn't help her, she will be angry – not solely because he didn't help her, but also because of her assumption. Her assumption could be 100% correct, but it could also be only 20% correct or not true at all. Our anger rises up and fits into the 'slot' of our basic assumption.

We stop being angry by making sure we are thinking correctly about the situation. I stop myself being angry (when I do stop myself) by rethinking the situation, by changing my thoughts about the incident. One of the main reasons we become angry with others is because of our 'shoulds'. 'He should know when I need help,' thinks the wife above. 'I shouldn't have to ask for help every time.' Maybe she is right, but it is the 'should' statement that is making her angry. Or she may be wrong; he may really not be able to recognise when she needs help. Or he may be lazy and is pretending. Or any of a dozen other reasons. Coming to an understanding of this one area of this couple's life will help anger from forming and from being expressed on that theme.

Charlene was wrong about her parents. When she realised the source of her anger at them and was able to talk to them about it, they were shocked. They had not realised how their behaviour had affected her. She was wrong about them because they were extremely proud of her and loved her very much. Their behaviour was wrong, but, just as in the story of the prodigal son, they had focused on the problem child to the extent that they made Charlene feel unappreciated and unloved. They deliberately changed their behaviour and Charlene gradually lost her resentment towards them.

Forgiveness

Ultimately, forgiveness is the antidote for anger. After there has been an understanding of the problem, after finding out why one is angry, if bitterness still lingers, the only solution is to forgive. Forgiveness melts anger; true forgiveness works every time; forgiveness taps into the power of love and takes away bitterness. Remaining angry is a power drainer; anger drains us of positive power. Forgiveness is a power filler; it fills us with the power of love. When we repent, no matter how horrible we have been, God forgives us. And he demands that we do the same for others, he demands that we forgive them when they repent (Matthew 6:14).

Easy you say, easy to forgive someone when they come to us and beg for our forgiveness. But what about the times when they do not? What about the times they insist they were right, or ignore the problem, or just go away out of our life? What are we to do with our anger then?

As a psychologist and as a Christian, my answer is the same as above. If we are to rid ourselves of anger, we must ultimately forgive. Anger is very damaging to our lives; it eats us up inside; it drains us of power; it usually does the angry person much more harm than it does the one who has caused the anger. The negative power of anger keeps anyone who is experiencing it from growing, both emotionally and in their faith. It must be dealt with.

This can be done alone, by writing about it or thinking the problem through and coming to a deliberate decision to forgive. But it is far better if we can find someone to talk to about it; anger needs to be released and talking is a safe method of release. The 'listener' needs to be just that, however, a listener only. To go to someone with a problem of anger and have that person say something like 'You shouldn't be angry' is very discouraging. Maybe you should be angry; maybe there is an injustice that more people should be angry about. It is how one expresses that anger that is important; learning how to deal with one's anger in a manner that is not power draining is the goal. If

I am angry about the world letting children go hungry (which I am) and if I do nothing but stew about it, then I deserve to be drained of power. The energy of my anger needs to be turned into activism in order to be power filling rather than power draining.

If you are angry about something that can't be helped, if anger occurs because of something someone has said or done and you find yourself unable or unwilling to forgive, then talking through the incident or incidents which have made you angry, letting someone else 'carry your burden' will help. It may take many 'talking throughs'; once may not be enough, but it needs to be done, for emotional health as well as for spiritual health. Anything that drains us of power keeps us from experiencing the fullness of God's power.

As a married person, as well as a person who does marriage therapy, I often wonder how any marriage lasts without an understanding of the Christian concept of forgiveness. In marriage, if we each do not forgive all the petty annoyances that occur, life will be one long power struggle and the inner peace Christ promised us will simply be a dream. By experiencing Christ's forgiveness of me, I can then forgive others. I think that is hard to understand unless one has experienced this forgiveness of Christ. In work relationships, it is often not possible to talk to the person who has made you angry; you may be too far down on the continuum of power in relation to that person. If that is the case, then after unburdening yourself with one other person, the ultimate solution is to forgive. Forgive and get on with your life, having been freed to experience the fullness of God's power.

The next and last chapter is about this power, spiritual power, the most power-filling of all.

CHAPTER 10

SPIRITUAL POWER

Spiritual power is the utmost, the highest type of power we can experience. If we feel powerless or power empty, then spiritual power is the ultimate way to become power full. Why is this so? Because when we are touched spiritually, we are touched in our innermost core, our soul. Our soul, our inner spirit, is where inner peace, if we have it, exists. When something touches us and evokes either a calm, peaceful feeling or a tenderness that often brings tears, or near tears, we interpret this as emotion. It is emotion, but so are many other feelings and they do not bring this result. Music, art, a poignant scene, nature, there are many ways our soul can be touched. Whenever we feel that piercing flash, somewhere in the vicinity of the heart, we have been touched internally, in our spirit. In a very real way, these 'touchings' or fillings of power, as I would call them, are just a taste of what we need to become power full.

That is where God speaks to us, in our spirit, in our soul. The Bible tells us that God is love; in other words, he is the definition of love and love is the definition of God. He is the ultimate source of this love, this energy, this power. If we need to feel power full, it stands to reason we should turn to God for this. If power means love, if how we feel power full is by being loved, then the most loved we can be is by God. If we are able to experience the power of love on a human level, either through our children or through our parents or another relationship, then how much more must this power of love exist in God?

The following story graphically illustrates the act of receiving God's love.

Maya Angelou was asked to write a poem to commemorate the inauguration of President Bill Clinton. The poem was stirring, inspirational; it was about America and its people. Dr Angelou had already achieved much by this time. She was a noted college professor, author and lecturer; she was not a powerless person. Later, she was interviewed by Oprah Winfrey on her talk show. Oprah brought the conversation around to the inauguration. 'Was it one of your proudest moments?' Oprah asked. Maya answered in her slow, compassionate, measured tones and said that it was a great, proud moment. But she went on to say that some private revelations may be greater. 'I think the great moment in my life happened in 1953. I was with a teacher, Frederick Wilkerson, who was a voice teacher and also a spiritual teacher. And he had a number of students, opera singers, all white, and all very, very well known. And I was a dancer and just trying. And he stayed in my house; so he had those people come over, his favourites, come over every Saturday, and we would read the Bible and read lessons in truth. And it fell my turn to read. And I read "God loves me." And he said, "Read it again." And I said, "God loves me." And he said, "Read it again." And he was embarrassing me in front of all these people, these older, well known – I said, "God loves me." He said, "Now try to know it."'

There was a pause as she looked at Oprah, remembering

that moment. 'Oprah – Oprah, it still – I'm – the skies open up. I can do anything. Anything I want to do, anything good, anything helpful, I can do it. You see?' Oprah answered, 'Yes, I do.' And Maya said, 'That is the greatest moment.'[16] At that moment, Maya Angelou received more power than she had ever had. She became power full, she felt truly loved. It was not an intellectual moment; she felt loved by God.

As Christians, we believe God's love for the world was shown by sending his Son, Jesus Christ, to die for our sins. For many, the experience of coming to know Christ is the first time in their lives they have felt truly loved. Conversion stories always have some element of euphoria; in fact, when people tell of their experiences, it is hard to distinguish the description of their feelings from those of someone who has just fallen in love. Little wonder; love is love. The situations should sound similar because the feelings would naturally be the same, although stronger, and with the added element of the miraculous. Somehow, in ways none of us can fully understand, this love infuses us, surrounds us, envelops us.

Even those who have had loving relationships in the past, those who have them now, who are not empty – they also benefit from this ultimate power. In other words, no matter how power full we are, there is more power to be obtained; the power which connects us to Christ is more fulfilling, more power full than any other kind of power. And further, I believe that deep within each of us is an empty space, a space that will be empty until it has been filled with a personal knowledge of Christ. Many people cannot identify it; they do not know what it is they are seeking, but they know that empty space is there. I believe we all search for Christ, we just do not always know that Christ is what we are looking for.

If one is searching, the natural thing to do is to go to

church. Great comfort can be derived from attending church, serving the church, etc., but someone can do those things for years and never really know what receiving Christ's love, Christ's power is about. I know; I was one of those people.

My story

My parents did not go to church and there was no evidence of spirituality in my home. Because of my father's job, we lived in Guatemala from the time I was four until I was seven, where, because of the affordability of servants, I had a nursemaid who did nothing but take care of me. Olga was the fourteen-year-old daughter of our cook; I spent all my time with her and she seemed to me to be very grown up. Some time during those three years, we lived in a rural area where there was a small chapel across the road from our house. Olga and I often went there, kneeling in front of the ornate, golden altar. When our family came back to the United States, we moved every year because my father worked for the US Army, building runways. Wherever we lived, I would ask to go to Sunday school. I would go alone or may have been escorted (I don't remember) to whatever church was within walking distance. I never thought it strange that I should ask to go, but now, looking back as an adult, I feel very sorry for that little girl; it seems to me to have been a very lonely thing to do. I do know that I wished we were a 'normal' family; I wanted us all to go, like the other children's parents. I was incredibly shy and never got to settle down in one place long enough to get over my shyness. So the fact that I asked and went by myself is remarkable, totally out of my character. It had to be the Holy Spirit drawing me.

After I married and had children, my husband and I

joined the Episcopal Church. At last, I could now say I was something! I was an Episcopalian, no longer a wanderer; it felt good to belong somewhere. I enjoyed the liturgical service; I loved to kneel; the entire atmosphere seemed to me to be 'holy'. It was only recently that I remembered Olga and myself kneeling and realised that was probably why I was drawn to a church where one kneels. I felt I was in a holy place, worshipping, but I still did not know what was going·on. I thought there was some big mystery that I didn't understand and that if I just kept coming Sunday after Sunday, maybe I would find out what it was. I also thought I was the only one who did not understand this mystery. I had been to all the classes that taught me about the Episcopal faith; I even read the Bible every now and then. I was drawn and yet I could not have told you why I was there, except that it was good to put your children in Sunday school and good to go with them and besides, I always felt better after I had been to church.

Then came my crisis. It was 1968, during the Vietnam War. My husband, like many civilians, had been drafted into the military and we were stationed on an Air Force base in Mobile, Alabama. I had been very unhappy in my marriage for a long time. I began awakening in the morning with crying spells, having no idea what I was crying about, the tears just seemed to flow of their own accord. I was not a psychologist then and I knew nothing about depression. Now, looking back, I can understand that I was clinically depressed. I finally decided I had to have help and rather than going to a therapist, I chose to see a minister instead.

The chaplain on the base listened to my story, to my symptoms, letting me do most of the talking. When he finally spoke, I was to be very disappointed. 'I have had training in Freudian psychology,' he told me. 'I want to begin to regress you back to age four and we will find out what is bothering you.' He said I was to begin taking Valium and that I would soon be feeling better. No mention had been made of prayer, or Christ, or healing. I sat there, stunned, then became angry. 'Look,' I said, 'I have been going to church for years and I have never before asked for help. This is my hour of need, and if Christianity has no power, then I'm going to start going sailing on Sunday mornings!'

He looked at me as if he wanted to pat me on the head and say, 'Now, now, dear.' I went home after having made another appointment for the following week; I was desperate and didn't know where else to turn. I began taking Valium and got through the second session, still wondering if Christianity did have any power. By the third session, he told me he had some bad news; he was being transferred soon and did not want to get in too deep with me and then have to leave. 'Since you are an Episcopalian,' he said, 'I'm referring you to an Episcopal priest in town. He works part-time at a mental health centre.'

I waited a couple of weeks and then went to see this priest, having absolutely no expectations this time. I assumed it would be the same kind of help I was receiving, totally secular. However, the minute I walked into Ed Lakeman's office, I knew something was different about him; he seemed to exude peace, calm, kindness. He listened to my story, said absolutely nothing about it, and then began to tell me his story. 'I have been a priest for twelve years,' he said, 'and I've only been a Christian for a year.' This shocked me; I had never heard any clergy of any denomination say anything like this. What did he mean? He must have been a Christian, else how could he have gone to seminary; how could he have held services and given sermons all these years? He must be a Christian – just as I was.

Ed had been converted, 'born again', come to know what it was all about – in other words, received Christ's love and power – the year before. An evangelist for Teen Challenge had come to Mobile, had met Ed, and could tell after talking to him that he really did not know Christ. He prayed with Ed to receive Jesus Christ, and so, at long last, Ed Lakeman, the priest, came into a relationship with his Saviour. After he had finished his dramatic story, he read a few passages from the Bible, prayed for me, and said, 'You probably won't need to come back. I will be out of town next week anyway, but if you want to come back, I'll see you then.'

I did feel better than when I had arrived, but I attributed it to the fact that I had cried a lot, which always makes one feel better. However, the next morning, everything was different. I awoke feeling wonderful, euphoric, as if I were wrapped in a soft, warm, pink cloud (I had discarded the Valium by then). Not only that, but I had an intense desire to read the Bible, something I had never experienced. I was reading in John's Gospel, reading passages that were fairly familiar to me, passages I had heard over and over again in church. Not only did I understand them in a way I never understood before, the words appeared to have a dimensional effect, much the way 3-D pictures do. It was as if there were words within words. It was a very supernatural event, yet I had no fear; my only emotion was wonder.

These good feelings and desire to read the Bible lasted for three days. Then everything went away, just like that! I could hardly wait for the priest to get back in town; I went to see him as soon as I could get an appointment, told him my story in a breathless rush and asked, 'What happened to me?' He did not seem shocked or alarmed; he just smiled and said, 'The Holy Spirit was with you.' 'But he went away!' I said. 'Well, you're lucky he was with you that long,' he answered, laughing. He went on to explain that everyone doesn't have dramatic conversion experiences and that for some people who do, it is just a moment in time. 'You were very blessed that those feelings lasted that long.' I remembered reading somewhere about Billy Graham having a conversion experience and of course, there are the stories about saints, 'special people'. I had never personally known anyone or at least no one had shared with me a personal conversion experience. I guess I thought these things were extraordinary, out of my grasp, not for such as me. I didn't dare tell anyone; I was almost afraid to tell this priest. If he hadn't acted so spiritual when I first saw him, rather than secular, I am sure I would have been hesitant to tell him. As I look back on it, it seems incredible to me that when those feelings of being loved and being drawn to the Bible happened to me, I honestly did not understand what was happening.

What had happened was that I had received Christ's power, Christ's love. I had not asked for it; I did not know how to ask for it, other than to tell the first minister that if Christianity had no power I was not going to come to church any more. Christ knew I was searching and in that respect, I was seeking whatever Christ had to give me. My experience with the Holy Spirit was the beginning of my becoming power full. That is what the Holy Spirit does, he fills us with power (Acts 1:8).

Yet there are many believers who do not feel power full. They go to church, attend prayer meetings, study the Bible, do good works, and serve on endless committees. They may even be vicars, wives and husbands of vicars, yes – dare I say it – bishops! How could this be?

One reason is that some have never received the Holy Spirit. They are believers in Christ, have been baptised in the name of the Lord Jesus, but have never experienced the fullness of the Trinity. We are told in Acts chapter nineteen about believers in Ephesus. '[Paul] asked them, "Did you receive the Holy Spirit when you believed?" They answered, "No, we have not even heard that there is a Holy Spirit"' (Acts 19:2).

In many churches today, there is little mention of the Holy Spirit. Christ said, 'You will receive power when the Holy Spirit comes on you' (Acts 1:8). If the place God speaks to us is in our soul, then the method is by the Holy Spirit. The power that comes from the Holy Spirit is far too seldom spoken of. Some are wary of preaching or hearing about the Holy Spirit because they have a fear and/or a prejudice against the practice of speaking in tongues. Yet neither Christ nor Paul nor anyone else in the Bible said that everyone who receives the Holy Spirit would necessarily speak in tongues. That gift is simply one of the gifts of the Spirit. There are many gifts of the Spirit, the gift of healing, the gift of being able to help others, the gift of administration, to name a few. No one knows which gifts are going to be given to him or her. But few could turn down the prospect of power, as promised in Acts. Knowing that one is loved by God and being filled with the power of the Holy Spirit is the ultimate way to become power full. An intellectual belief in Jesus is not enough. ⇐

I must add a cautionary note here, lest some readers may think the 'power' of the Holy Spirit is an end in itself. Salvation, knowing one is forgiven after repenting and asking Christ for forgiveness, giving one's self and life over to Christ and from there, receiving the Holy Spirit, from whom power is given, is the goal. Simon, a sorcerer, was baptised and believed in Jesus 'and he followed Philip everywhere, astonished by the great signs and miracles he saw' (Acts 8:13). This man was a magician and had amazed people with the things he did. He was so impressed by watching the apostles lay hands on believers in order for them to receive the Holy Spirit that he tried to give the apostles some money, asking them to 'give me also this ability so that everyone on whom I lay my hands may receive the Holy Spirit' (Acts 8:19). Simon wanted the power – not the kind of power I've been speaking of throughout this book; not the power of love, not a power that fills one up, but a power to show signs and miracles. This can be a manifestation of the Holy Spirit, but when I say that knowing one is truly loved by God and being filled with the power of the Holy Spirit is the ultimate way to be power full, I am speaking of the inward filling of the Holy Spirit, the inward, internal knowledge that God loves me – knowledge given by the Holy Spirit.

Peace

> Jesus said, 'Peace I leave with you; my peace I give you. I do not give to you as the world gives. Do not let your hearts be troubled and do not be afraid'.
>
> (John 14:27)

Here it is! That inner peace I have been speaking of through the entire book. The pursuit of peace, rather than happiness. Christ promised those who believed in him they would experience peace. Yet look at the next line: 'Do not let your hearts be troubled and do not be afraid.' He did not say, 'I will not let your hearts be troubled; I will not let you be afraid.' Jesus is speaking of something we must do, actively do, not just let it happen to us.

There are many believers who do not experience this peace. It seems to me it is because they 'let their hearts be troubled and are afraid'. Afraid of illness, of poverty, of business deals falling through, of children not behaving as they should. If we are not trusting God to take care of us, it is because we have not yet turned our lives over to him; we are still struggling.

Power struggles

Not only do we need to be filled with the Holy Spirit, we also need to turn our lives over to Christ in order that he can 'remake' us. Ironically, turning one's life over to Christ can be a bigger power struggle than any we experience. The struggle is both within ourselves (inner action) and with Christ (interaction). We may rebel against anyone (Supreme Being or no) having power over us, and thus we do not submit; we struggle. In the spiritual sense, unless we let Christ exert power over us, we receive few benefits; it is just intellectual belief. Just believing in Christ is comforting; being filled with the Spirit is power filling, but if there is an ongoing struggle, we cannot attain inner peace. How do we struggle with Christ? By how we use our free will.

Free will

One of the mysterious contradictions in the life of faith is that we have been given free will and yet we must submit our will to a higher Being. Free will is the most generous gift we could have been given by God and yet this same free will is what gets us into trouble. Free will is power; either negative power or positive power, negative energy or positive energy. We have the free will to get angry, to hate, to love or to forgive. It is our choice. After receiving Christ's love and power, our independent free will is still there; without free will we would not be able to make decisions, either for ourselves or for others. Without free will we would be reduced to automatons. Without free will there would be no power struggle either within ourselves or with Christ; we would probably do the right thing all the time. But instead of creating a world full of holy, obedient robots, God chose to give us the right to choose. We get to choose whether to believe, we get to choose how to behave, and we even get to choose whether to struggle with God or not.

Believers in Christ know, in differing degrees, that obeying Christ, submerging one's free will, will bring ultimate inner peace. Yet we keep on not doing it; we keep on being self-destructive. Why? For the same reason we don't do all the other things we know we are supposed to do; for the same reason we don't love as much as we could, for the same reason we don't do as much for others as we could. We are basically self-serving human beings and in our constant struggle for happiness, we want our own way. Just as we want our own way in our earthly relationships, so is it with our relationship to Christ.

Turning our free will over to Christ also sounds very scary. There is a prevailing myth that teaches 'if you turn your life over to Christ, he will test you, put you through fiery trials; you might get cancer or lose a loved one – just so Christ can see how you handle it'. For those outside religious communities, I am sure this sounds very strange. It is strange; it is strange that we make Christ such an ogre and even if we do not voice these fears, usually have them somewhere in the back of our mind. If we turn over our free will (the power we do have), then might not Christ simply 'do us in'?!

Turn in the road

Here, again, is the turn in the road. As I said in the first chapter, if our goal from the beginning had been inner peace rather than happiness, we would not have so much trouble giving up our free will to Christ. It is easy to understand that human beings might not trust Christ to make them happy. After all, some of the things we want that we think would make us happy are very unspiritual and probably not in line with Christ's will. We think that this or that will make us happy, then when we get this or that, we are not happy. So we begin to wonder what *will* make us happy? Only inner peace, inner peace that is obtained by becoming power full and obeying Christ.

You see, giving Christ power over our lives does not drain us of power. The more we give to Christ, the more we receive. Christ fills us with the power of positive emotions, love, peace, joy, contentment, but we must trust him and give up the power struggle.

I, like many others I know, am still seeking permanent peace. It is a daily struggle between what I know I should do and what my free will (the negative part of it) does, almost seemingly against my will. But I do experience peace a great deal of the time and I no longer actively seek happiness. I now know that writing this book, or buying something wonderful, or seeing a land I have always wanted to see will only bring transitory happiness.

What I strive for now is inner peace. I can get that peace by giving up trying to get power from things and from trying to control others. I can get that peace by seeking power in terms of living a loving life, by asking not what others can do for me, but what I can do for them. I have access to Christ's power, but it is up to me whether to receive it and/or whether to use it. I imagine that this inner struggle will always be present, in all of us, to greater or lesser degrees. All I know at this point is that this peace is much more lasting and fulfilling than happiness.

Endings and beginnings

As this book comes to an end, I hope that understanding the concepts of the *Powerdigm* theory helped you to become power full and at the very least, to understand why you feel and act as you do.

If you have learned to identify the cause of those empty feelings, if you can now label what drains you of power and conversely, what fills you up, if you realise the dynamics of power struggles and can understand how your behaviour affects those relationships, then you will have gained something useful from reading this book. If you know that anger and resentment, addictions, anxiety, depression and all other negative emotions block our way, detour our journey through life, and if putting these very human emotions into the *Powerdigm* theory is helpful, then the purpose of this book has been accomplished.

Remember, inner peace is the goal we should all seek, rather than happiness. Happiness is fickle and transitory, but inner peace, attained by becoming power full, is wondrously lasting.

NOTES

1 *The Alternative Service Book 1980* (Oxford University Press: Oxford, and A. R. Mowbray & Co. Ltd.: Oxford, 1980), p. 200.

2 Joe Morgan, the baseball star, was interviewed on National Public Radio *Fresh Air* (name of the programme) by host, Terry Gross.

3 Cousins, Norman, *Anatomy of an Illness as Perceived by the Patient: Reflections on Healing and Regeneration* (Norton: New York, 1979).

4 Lewis, C. S., *All My Road Before Me: The Diary of C. S. Lewis* (Harcourt, Brace & Company: San Deigo, CA, 1979).

5 Lewis, C. S., *Surprised by Joy* (Fount: London, 1955).

6 *Haus am Checkpoint Charlie* (Bureau, Publisher, Archives, Filmstudio and Museum: Berlin).

7 Quintanilla, Michael, 'The Dean of Dreams', *Los Angeles Times*, 6 December 1993, pp. E1 and E3.

8 *The NIV Study Bible* (Zondervan Corporation: 1985), p. 1798.

9 Kolodny, Nancy J., *When Food's a Foe: How to Confront and Conquer Eating Disorders* (Little, Brown & Company: USA, 1987).

10 Silverstein, Alvin, Virginia and Robert, *The Addictions Handbook* (Enslow Publishers Inc.: Hillside, NJ, 1991), p. 42.

11 *Ibid.*, p. 43.

12 *Ibid.*, pp. 28–30.

13 Burns, David, *Feeling Good* (Avon Books: New York, 1992), p. 42.

14 Barclay, William, *The Daily Study Bible, Gospel of Matthew, Volume 1* (The Saint Andrew Press: Edinburgh, 1956), pp. 138–139.

15 Barclay, William, *The Daily Study Bible, The Letters to the Galatians and Ephesians* (The Saint Andrew Press: Edinburgh, 1954), pp. 184–185.

16 *Oprah Winfrey Show*, transcript.

Jayne Lind is available for seminars and talks regarding this book. She also would like to hear from you if you have an interesting story about becoming power full. Please write to:

> Jayne Lind
> PO Box 216
> Bury St. Edmunds
> Suffolk
> IP28 6LJ

The author regrets that she is unable to answer letters about personal problems.

Personality Plus – the book which could change your life for the better!

- ◼ *Understand how your personality affects your emotions, work performance and relationships*

- ◼ *Grow stronger by overcoming personal weaknesses*

- ◼ *Become confident in achieving your full potential for a fulfilling life*

- ◼ *Discover valuable insights into your unique, God-given nature*

"Excellent . . . I laughed my way through this absorbing book and discovered at the end just how much I had learnt about other people – and myself!

Jennifer Rees Larcombe

Personality Plus
Florence Littauer
ISBN 1 85424 299 7

Available from your local Christian Bookshop.
In case of difficulty contact Monarch Books,
Concorde House, Grenville Place, Mill Hill, London NW7 3SA

MONARCH
B O O K S

Your Personality and the Spiritual Life

A self-help resource book for understanding your personality and how it can affect your relationship with God and others.

- *Ideas for devotional patterns that are best suited to your personality*

- *It will enable God to enrich your personality and use you even more fully than before*

- *Full of Biblical guidelines to help your spiritual growth*

Dr Reginald Johnson is Professor of Spiritual Formation at Asbury Theological Seminary in Wilmore, Kentucky. He is a frequent retreat leader and speaker at churches and conferences.

Your Personality and the Spiritual Life
Reginald Johnson
ISBN 1 85424 340 3

Available from your local Christian Bookshop.
In case of difficulty contact Monarch Books,
Concorde House, Grenville Place, Mill Hill, London NW7 3SA

MONARCH
BOOKS